Self-Help in the 1890s Depression

# Self-Help
## IN THE
# 1890s Depression

H. ROGER GRANT

*The Iowa State University Press*

AMES

FOR   MARTHA

Composed and printed by The Iowa State University Press
Ames, Iowa  50010

First edition, 1983

**Library of Congress Cataloging in Publication Data**

Grant, H. Roger, 1943–
  Self-help in the 1890s depression.

    Includes bibliographical references and index.
    1. United  States—Economic  conditions—1865–1918.  2.  Depressions—1893—United
States. 3. Self-help groups—United States—History. I. Title.
HC105.G82        1983        973.8′7        82–13054
**ISBN 0–8138–1634–3**

# Contents

PREFACE     vii

ACKNOWLEDGMENTS     xi

INTRODUCTION
*Hard Times*     3

CHAPTER ONE
*Community Gardens*     23

CHAPTER TWO
*Labor Exchange*     40

CHAPTER THREE
*Cooperative Stores*     59

CHAPTER FOUR
*Farmers' Railroads*     74

CHAPTER FIVE
*Intentional Communities*     101

AFTERWORD
*Self-Help Brought Up to Date*     128

NOTES     141

INDEX     159

# *Preface*

THE NEWS MEDIA OF LATE have repeatedly reported how Americans cope with "stagflation" and related financial problems. Seemingly, the notion exists that such self-help schemes as consumer-owned railroads and community gardens are either recent inventions or perhaps date only from the Great Depression of the 1930s or wartime experiences. Although scholars have not focused expressly on the origins of bootstrap proposals, published accounts reveal that the legacy is much older. Many self-help ideas were concocted or refined during the country's first major industrial depression, those troubled years between 1893 and 1897 when millions joined the ranks of the unemployed and underemployed.

While historians have studied with considerable care the depression of the thirties, the devastating economic dislocations of forty years before have not received the attention they deserve. I have several objectives in writing this book. I want to describe dimensions of the story of the hard times of the 1890s that have been left mostly untold and to suggest that the concept of self-help, so superbly reflective of Americans' age-old desire to be self-reliant, continues to have value. I also want to throw light on the gestation period of that great housecleaning escapade, the Progressive era. Admittedly, I am influenced considerably by David P. Thelen's *The New Citizenship: Origins of Progressivism in Wisconsin, 1885–1900.* In this pioneering study Thelen emphasizes the consumer thrust of emerging progressivism. The cataclysmic depression, triggered by the Panic of 1893, caused heretofore fragmented reform efforts to coalesce into a new crusade that enjoyed "cross-class" support. As Thelen describes the outlook of movement members: "They saw politics as a never-ending struggle between the aroused consumers and taxpayers ('the people') and a producer-oriented establishment that constantly thwarted the will of the majority."[1]

The theme of consumer resistance to acts of corporate arrogance explains much of the nature and overall impulse of progressivism. Yet the Thelen thesis, it seems, could include the experi-

vii

ences of self-help. Specifically, the togetherness spawned by efforts of the down-and-out to improve their immediate lot created bonds that were vital to subsequent political activities that saw the fusion of classes, "the people," against the business elite. The sense of oneness created by community gardens, for example, is nicely revealed by an unemployed Detroit stovemaker: "The citizens are getting to understand that they can make good changes if they know that they can achieve something. We garden together and save ourselves. . . . We can surely vote together and redeem the repub. for ourselves and make the cities and the states places where justice will forever reign." Attached to self-help plans were decidedly reform concepts designed to make permanent change—the stuff that was at the heart of progressivism. "While the people may believe that self-improvement projects like the vacant lot [community garden] program and these worker colonies are only to deal with today's needs," observed a St. Louis journalist, "they contain the germ of something much more vital for the future. . . . they are the beginnings of ideas and values that may well bring about a new morrow."[2]

In a related fashion my examination of self-help shows the bonds between populism and progressivism. After all, the fact that both movements were responses to industrialism is generally accepted. Certain bootstrap programs—most notably cooperatives and farmers' railroads—indicate that schemes either perfected or developed by Populists were subsequently embraced by those best labeled as Progressives. The linkage between the two is evident and displays the continuity in the annals of the origins of modern America.

This study of self-help nine decades ago also exhibits much about the character of the nation. Unquestionably, the impact of the work ethic is a central feature of these bootstrap efforts. But an equally important though less obvious trait is the do-it-now mentality; Americans have regularly been in a hurry. "Lost time," said *Poor Richard's Almanac,* "is never found again." Self-help offered instant or at least a speedy means of improvement. "I like gardens because they don't take that long to produce," explained a Denver "potato patch" participant. "It takes several seasons at best for a reform bill in our place or in the national capitol to ever get out of the hopper." Americans not only believed firmly in the value of toil—indeed swift toil—but they knew that solutions existed to the nagging problems of the day, even when the economy crashed as it never had before. During the nineties' depression Detroit Mayor Hazen S. Pingree, no dreamy idealist, said it well: "The problems of hard times can and will be solved. There is much of a personal and group method that can be done to bring relief that works well." While there were those who may have had their confidence badly shaken, the gut feeling prevailed that "people can overcome difficulties" and "self help is a way."[3]

In an attempt to understand the self-help phenomenon during the depression of the nineties and to relate it to the broader picture of reform during the period, I have selected five case studies. Community gardens, labor exchanges, cooperative stores, farmers' railroads, and intentional communities represent, in my estimation, the quintessential efforts at uplift. But before the core, there is a review of the hard times. An Afterword is also included that briefly carries the story of the individual episodes to the present.

# Acknowledgments

I WISH TO THANK PUBLICLY the individuals and institutions that have assisted me in the preparation of this study. Douglas W. Steeples of Westminster College in Salt Lake City indirectly helped to spark my interest in this subject. His masterful 1965 essay, "The Panic of 1893: Contemporary Reflections and Reactions," which appeared in *Mid-America,* caught my eye as a first-year graduate student at the University of Missouri. Since then Doug has become a friend and has shared with me his revised 1961 doctoral work, "Five Troubled Years: A History of the Depression of 1893–1897," which he wrote under the guidance of J. Carlyle Sitterson and George B. Tindall at the University of North Carolina. David P. Thelen, my dissertation coadvisor at Missouri, also drew me to the 1890s, especially the impact of the Panic of 1893 on American society. While I labored on the topic of insurance reform during the Populist-Progressive era under his tutelage, I knew that someday I might work specifically on the depression. I am also grateful to my colleagues at the University of Akron, particularly David Kyvig, Jerome Mushkat, Daniel Nelson, and James Richardson, for their continued support. And I want to recognize three others: Robert S. Fogarty of Antioch College for suggesting an interpretative framework in which to view utopian experiments of the late nineteenth century and for directing me to several archival sources; Viola Olerich Storms of Moline, Illinois, for sharing with me her memories and materials that relate to her utopian writer father, Henry Olerich; and Frank E. Vyzralek, former state archivist of North Dakota, for bringing the obscure farmers' railroad movement to my attention.

The staffs of the Baker Library, Harvard University, Cambridge; Colorado Historical Society, Denver; Burton Historical Collection, Detroit Public Library; Iowa State Historical Department, Division of the State Historical Society, Iowa City; Kansas State Historical Society, Topeka; Library of Congress, Washington, D.C.; Michigan Historical Collections, University of Michigan, Ann Arbor; Minnesota Historical Society, St. Paul; State Historical Society of Missouri, Columbia; Newberry Library, Chicago; New York Public Library, New York City; North Dakota Institute for Regional Studies, Fargo; State Historical Society of North Dakota, Bismarck; Ohio Historical Society, Columbus; Toledo–Lucas County Public Library, Toledo; and the Western Reserve Historical Society, Cleveland, provided essential and effective assistance. A Faculty Research Committee Grant and a Faculty Summer Research Fellowship from the University of Akron paid for much of my research expenses, including the costs of travel to those depositories.

Portions of this book have appeared in altered versions in several periodicals. I wish to thank the editors of *Colorado Magazine, Communal Societies, Detroit in Perspective, Kansas Historical Quarterly, Missouri Historical Society Bulletin,* and *North Dakota History* for granting me permission to use this material.

My typists made the writing immeasurably easier, and I want to express my appreciation to Garnette Dorsey and Dorothy Richards for their patience and efficiency. My wife, Martha Farrington Grant, assisted in numerous ways; most of all she read various drafts and offered useful criticisms. And lastly I thank my eight-year-old daughter, Julia Dinsmore Grant, for her complete indifference to this project. She left me mostly undisturbed for research and writing, but she would have helped if she could.

H.R.G.


*Akron, Ohio*

Self-Help in the 1890s Depression

# Hard Times

H E year 1893 was dreadful. It marked both the beginning of a long and deep depression and a time of severe economic crisis. "Never before has there been such a sudden and striking cessation of industrial activity," observed a critic in the September issue of the usually optimistic *Commercial and Financial Chronicle*. And this publication went on to summarize the extent of America's money woes: "Nor is any section of the country exempt from the paralysis; mills, factories, furnaces, mines nearly everywhere shut down in large numbers, and commerce and enterprise are arrested in an extraordinary degree. . . . and hundreds of thousands of men thrown out of employment." The early months of 1893 had given no clear warning of impending financial disaster. Yet for the observant, the national economy revealed signs of serious, even potentially fatal illness; indeed, the malaise was widespread.[1]

By the advent of the industrial dislocations of the mid-1890s, American agriculture had already encountered grave difficulties. Just as agrarians of the 1920s commonly felt "hard times" years before urbanites, their counterparts in the late 1880s similarly knew adversity before city folks. Two regions in particular faced economic troubles: the South and the Great Plains.

Since the Civil War the Southland had become an economic backwater. Ravages of the conflict, market disruptions, and soil exhaustion inflicted serious restrictions on the area's financial health. Although production of cotton, the region's leading cash crop, more than doubled between 1870 and 1890, weak and occasionally plummeting commodity prices crippled most producers. And the crop lien system totally trapped thousands who worked the land. Even though ubiquitous "furnishing merchants" offered credit that was often unobtainable elsewhere to the vast mudsill ele-

3

ment, borrowers paid an enormous price. Not only did the system humiliate them, but they regularly paid a ruinous rate of interest (frequently exceeding 100 percent annually) for this service. These country capitalists, pressured in turn by their northern and eastern sources of money, forced the continuation of the fiber economy, since it served their financial interests. Cotton enjoyed easy marketability and primarily nonperishable properties, posed limited shipping problems, and could not be consumed by the grower in its raw state.[2]

While Southerners endured a prolonged period of economic grief following the war, grain producers on the fertile western prairies experienced relative prosperity during the Gilded Age. After a brief market slump in the early seventies, wheat prices rose steadily, peaking in 1881–1882. But as this income began a constant decline toward ultimate collapse, increased demands for meat created a strong corn market, thus cushioning somewhat the financial blow. Unlike the South, on the Plains mortgage money remained plentiful and interest rates reasonable for approximately a decade beginning in the middle seventies. Understandably, land booms occurred; the future seemed rosy.[3]

The bubble burst in 1887. Three successive droughts, a series of severe winters, diastrously low wheat and corn prices, and accelerating deflation meant bankruptcies and grinding mortgage levels for seemingly countless farmers and townspeople. Examples abound. In Kansas between 1889 and 1893, 11,122 farms were foreclosed, and in fifteen counties alone credit companies owned more than three-quarters of the land. In Saratoga, Kansas, a correspondent for the *New York Tribune* reported that there "stands an opera house which cost $30,000 to build and a $20,000 school house, as well as a substantial brick hotel and yet in that city there is not a single man to claim a thing as his own." In neighboring Nebraska an official of the mighty Burlington Railroad estimated in early 1891 that nearly a quarter of the infant villages along his firm's trackage "are virtually abandoned or soon will be." The agricultural depression threatened to turn scores of farming towns into sepulchers filled with dead bones and hopes.[4] All could appreciate the contemporary poetry of agrarian Will Carlton:

> We worked through spring and winter, through summer
>     and through fall
> But the mortgage worked the hardest and steadiest of them all;
> It worked on nights and Sundays, it worked each holiday;
> It settled down among us and never went away. . . .

And there came a dark day on us when the interest wasn't paid,
And there came a sharp foreclosure, and I kind o' lost my hold,
And grew weary and discouraged and the farm was cheaply sold.
The children left and scattered, when they hardly yet were grown; . . .

My wife she pined and perished, an' I found myself alone,
What she died of was a mystery, and the doctors never knew;
But I know she died of mortgage—just as well as I wanted to.[5]

Ominous clouds gathered on the business horizon. The agricultural calamity damaged the industrial sector. When tens of thousands of farmers curtailed their buying, many concerns suffered; agricultural conditions shaped in large measure the economy's expansion or contraction. The railroads, for one, saw their earnings drop sharply. Carriers, especially those that operated in depressed, rural territories, commonly responded by shelving expansion plans and slashing services. An illustration is South Dakota, a state dominated by two powerful Granger roads, the Chicago, Milwaukee and St. Paul (Milwaukee) and the Chicago and North Western. The Milwaukee ended its initial wave of track laying in 1887, after fifteen years of continuous building. The North Western stopped installing rails in 1890, terminating eighteen years of feverish construction. Yet the state's rail network remained incomplete; no route had pierced the vast region west of the Missouri River, and even in the East scores of "inland" communities awaited the iron horse to shatter their isolation. Furthermore, the two companies chopped off freight and passenger runs, closed depots, and fired or furloughed hundreds of employees, "trimming their working forces [by 1891] down to mere skeletons of their usual strength." Moreover, the Milwaukee and North Western both reduced local newspaper advertising, curtailed the use of complimentary annual and trip passes; and most important, began to dodge property taxes and other financial commitments.[6]

Before America's 1893 panic the financial storms already had struck abroad. Depression came to Germany in January 1890, and economic stagnation reigned there for the next five years. A much deeper slide and for a comparable duration hit England that September, triggered by the collapse of Baring Brothers, an investment house crippled by heavy losses in Argentine securities. And France experienced its "La Grand Dépression" starting in January 1891; full-scale recovery did not begin for the French until 1895.[7]

Not surprisingly the European crisis buffeted the American

economy. Foreign investors, particularly the English, liquidated a full range of securities; in the same vein, the outside flow of capital virtually ceased. Although stock traders experienced tense days, catastrophe was averted. Still, an overall contraction occurred. Economic activity in the United States slipped after July 1890, bottoming out during May the next year and then peaking in January 1893. The latter upswing was related directly to the European wheat famine in 1891, which for Americans fortunately coincided with a bountiful grain harvest. Even with lucrative agricultural exports, industrial activity remained nearly 10 percent below capacity and was generally unable to overcome the impact of bad times overseas.[8]

Prelude to panic came during the early months of 1893. The first startling event took place on February 20, when a major eastern trunk carrier, the Philadelphia and Reading, failed. Not only were its shares "smashed to smithereens" but securities of several other railroads dropped dramatically. Wall Street experienced its biggest volume of trade ever. An uneasy calm returned to the financial world, due mostly to the newly installed Grover Cleveland administration. This hard-money regime seemed sincerely concerned about the health of the economy and assumed a solid probusiness stance. Notwithstanding the confidence capitalists placed in the White House, the decline of the Treasury Department's gold reserve below the long-established $100 million minimum on April 22 caused massive anxiety. The country's increasingly shaky economy together with the on-going dislocations in Europe produced the metal drain.[9]

Fear turned to frenzy during the first week of May. As a *New York Times* headline on May 4 correctly reported, "A Great Day for the Bears in Wall Street," for a selling wave pounded the market. "Not since 1884 had the stock market had such a break in prices as occurred yesterday [May 3], and few days in its history were more exciting." A gigantic failure sparked the fall: the National Cordage Company entered receivership. This most active stock dropped fifteen points, a 30 percent loss in a single day of trading, and it continued to slide.[10]

The demise of National Cordage caused enormous psychological damage. This particular firm symbolized the new type of industrial concern that had come into prominence since the late eighties—the trust. A speculatively managed company, National Cordage had tried to exercise a tight grip on the production of twine, rope, and bagging by securing a virtually complete monopoly of the world's supply of manila hemp. In January 1893 it had paid a 100 percent dividend, but its free-wheeling antics soon brought failure.[11]

Panic spread. No security seemed immune, and bank closures became commonplace. In the week following the National Cordage debacle a host of brokerage firms failed and two prominent Chicago financial institutions closed their doors. Confidence and credit vanished; the economy sank in irretrievable collapse.[12]

Hard times haunted Americans for five years. The economic annals of this depression, however, reveal peaks and valleys, ones that most citizens probably failed to perceive. After the May and June rout, contraction continued until the following summer. Although the industrial and commercial dullness finally reached bottom, subsequent improvements did not produce recovery; the economy, with few exceptions, remained sluggish. Then another downturn occurred. The widespread fear of war with Great Britain, prompted largely by President Cleveland's belligerent message to Congress on December 17, 1895, that blasted British policy in the Venezuelan boundary dispute, sent stock prices tumbling. Continued worries about international and domestic matters generated still another period of stagnation. Not until the summer of 1897 did the economy exhibit clear-cut evidence of recovery. Only after the turn of the twentieth century did hard times become merely unpleasant memories.[13]

THE ECONOMIC SCOPE of the depression of the 1890s was staggering; American business enterprise lay in shambles. Soon after the panic, the nature of the disaster began to emerge. By September 1893, 172 state banks, 177 private ones, and forty-seven savings and loan associations had closed; by October, 158 national banks had folded; and by year's end company failures totaled a whopping 15,242. Prominent casualties included Oliver Iron and Steel; Atchison, Topeka and Santa Fé; and Union Pacific. During the summer twelve of the largest ore steamers on the Great Lakes never left their home ports, while many mine operators were wiped out by the hard times. "Factories are shut everywhere," became an oft-repeated description of the dramatic economic decline.[14]

Unemployment figures, perhaps a better barometer, reached all-time highs, and on a per capita basis during the winter of 1893–

1894 were likely the greatest in the nation's history. Admittedly, unemployment data are incomplete, but a "guestimation" of the out-of-work in eight leading manufacturing states by 1894 exceeds 23 percent. Pennsylvania, New York, and Michigan seemed especially hard hit, with unemployment 25, 35, and 43.6 percent, respectively. Certain industries felt the economic dislocations acutely. During the early months about 40 percent of the labor force in iron manufacturing experienced unemployment and over half of the woolen workers knew enforced idleness. The building trades faced universal paralysis. "Carpenters, brick masons, stone workers, plasterers, and various other crafts dependent upon finding work in house construction," reported the *Review of Reviews* in January 1894, "are experiencing not the usual three or four months' leisure out of twelve, but five or six months of inactivity, with no very good prospects before them." At the depth of the "workless winter" of 1893–1894, approximately 4.5 million individuals understood hard times intimately. Others, certainly a large portion of the country's 63 million residents, encountered drastic wage cuts or entered the ranks of the poorly paid underemployed. Clearly the country was troubled by unemployment that many thought was endemic.[15]

The human misfortune and suffering have not been truly appreciated. While the desperate plight of workers at Pullman and Cripple Creek is generally known, the stories of millions of anonymous Americans remain largely untold. One account from January 1894 that captures the intensity of the national catastrophy speaks of New York City, the nation's largest metropolis: "The enormous number of 55,000 men, women and girls, formerly employed in the clothing trade alone, are out of work, and consequently in want. Unskilled labor is at the starvation point." Added the report, "It is the same in all the large cities." Similarly, the *Arena* noted in March that "Thousands of men are stalking the streets of our cities searching, in vain, for employment and starvation stares their wives and children in the face." Residents of small industrial and mining towns confronted comparable difficulties. In the soft-coal fields of southern Iowa and northern Missouri depression struck with a vengeance. Demands for locomotive fuel dropped dramatically after the Panic of 1893 and the diggings, frequently railroad controlled, closed. In late winter 1895 an Ottumwa, Iowa, journalist described life in the nearby Appanoose County camp of Cincinnati: "The 500 mine families in this locality are in the most destitute circumstances. They have little to eat in the way of wholesome food and their clothing, if it can be called that, is in utter tatters. All have that sickly appearance. Many have been confined to bed with illness." And death stalked Cincinnati. "When persons die, their bodies are placed in home-made coffins and the men in the community dig the graves. I am told that there has been an unusually high rate of deaths, particularly among the children and babies, since these hard times began. The incidents of suicide have become almost commonplace." The reporter concluded with these thoughts: "The enforced idleness is taking a harsh toll on the living. I can see it after only a few moments. Perhaps the year will bring back jobs and hope for the future."[16]

Farmers, too, faced personal disaster. Even though many from the South and Great Plains had endured hardships for years, by 1894 conditions had reached the crisis stage. One agricultural paper told of the sorry state of affairs on the southern prairies. "Owing to drouths since the Cherokee strip [in Oklahoma] opened in 1893, no crops have been raised. Settlers have no resources to exist on, and to make the situation more desperate and hopeless they can not get away. The territorial government has no money to assist them."[17] Hundreds of miles to the north an officer of the Custer County Bank in Sargent, Nebraska, wrote an Iowa cousin in January 1895 the following description of local affairs:

> It is enough to make me heartsick to look at this once prosperous country. The suffering is terrible. There are bushes and cow chips enough to keep fires going, but flour and meal is what we want. We have several families who for a month past have had nothing to eat but flour and water and they are very thankful to get that. Scores of women and children have to stay in their sod shanties bare footed for the want of something to cover their feet. All this was brought on these people through no fault of theirs. They are hard working, industrious people; the shiftless and lazy hangers on to the community, together with a good many good citizens, were driven out by the drouth of 1890 and the following dry years. . . . The county is trying to do all it can, but we are so much in debt that it is next to impossible to get any one to take our warrants. . . . We are compelled to put our pride aside and ask aid, immediate aid; anything to eat or wear.[18]

Autopsies of industrial depression regularly reveal an initial stage characterized by shock and bewilderment. The depression of the nineties fits the pattern. During the formative period of the downswing, a sense of disbelief commonly permeated the writings of those who bothered to comment. "This strange condition of affairs—this distress in the midst of plenty—this superabundance of laborers and of the machinery of production, ready for employment, but unable to find it," are the words of Bostonian Uriel H. Crocker in the autumn of 1893. More pointed, a Tampa, Florida, merchant groaned, "I do not believe what has happened to my life and livelihood. . . . the country and I is doomed." People seemed stunned, and few expressed a rebellious mood.[19]

A widespread fear accompanied the initial shakeup. The unexpected turn in the economy caused an unsettling effect. A government employee warned his Fairmont, Minnesota, sweetheart, "Don't go out into the Country on your bycile [sic] . . . it is not safe. Those Tramps are getting desperate and every day are worse." While some spoke of the possibility of drifters attacking vulnerable cyclists, impending revolution dominated the thoughts of others. Was America on the verge of European-like class warfare? "If members of the unemployed continue to increase in the future," reflected a Cleveland, Ohio, newspaper in August 1893, "there is danger that the predictions of Lord Macaulay [the famed English historian of the Revolution of 1688] will come true. He predicted that the American republic would be over-thrown by vandals raised within her own borders; and if we consider that [Commissioner of Labor] Carroll D. Wright's last report gave the number of unemployed as over 2,000,000 (which would make a larger army than any the world ever saw), it is not hard to discern that a time may come when hunger and involuntary idleness will result in the forming of military organizations by the unemployed." In the same vein the editor of the *Twentieth Century Farmer* foresaw either "submission to the conditions of hopeless poverty or a bloody revolution."[20]

Soon anger largely replaced the shock and fear. After a year of so of hard times a new type of civic mind-set developed; one that gave birth to that great wave of national housecleaning called progressivism. The badly fragmented reform efforts of the Gilded Age started to coalesce into a crusade that—except for the business elite—crossed class lines. Depressed conditions brought this dramatic realignment. Most of all, citizens resented the tax dodging of the wealthy and especially the quasi-public corporations. They perceived the powerful as manipulating the tax system to widen the gap between the rich and poor and to place the heaviest financial burdens on the financially disadvantaged. "The tax dodger, by evading his due share of the public burden, either defrauds the revenues of his city, county and state or compels men of more honesty and generally of less property to bear a part of his load," observed a small-town Missouri editor. "In other words, he defrauds his fellow citizens, conscientiously; he has money in his possession that belongs to them. When companies evade their rightful responsibilities, the negative effect on the public is greatly compounded."[21]

Popular displeasure centered on business practices generally. In periods of financial stringency, firms often reduced services and raised rates. For example, in September 1895 alone, residents of the Wisconsin communities of Ashland, Fond du Lac, Superior, and Waukesha battled their water companies for failure to provide a healthful product at a fair cost. Such arbitrary actions by corporations were customarily viewed as arrogant; citizens expressed little sympathy for the corporate plight. While little was accomplished politically at this time, the depression served as the prime catalyst that ultimately led to programs of strict regulation or even government ownership of a variety of concerns, particularly units of the utilities industry.

As the reform movement started to spread at the grass-roots level, the depression era witnessed a scramble for the adoption of conflicting remedies at the federal level. Unmistakably, debate on three singularly different approaches proved a contributing factor in the ascendancy of the Republican party after 1896.

GROVER CLEVELAND had the distinct misfortune to be the occupant of the White House when economic calamity struck. Yet he thought he knew the proper response. While neither historian nor economist, the president realized that during the nineteenth century financial panics had occurred about once a decade and that a general lack of public confidence commonly fueled decline. Throughout his administration he believed that the panic had been *psychological* and stemmed directly from the business community's all-pervasive fear of an unstable currency.

The president longed for a true gold standard. He had absolutely no use for the mildly inflationist Sherman Silver Purchase Act. This 1890 measure provided for the monthly acquisition by the Treasury Department of 4.5 million ounces of silver for which the government issued legal tender notes redeemable in coin. Cleveland objected strongly to paper currency exchangeable for the yellow metal. As long as adequate supplies of gold remained in public vaults, conservative financiers and creditors expressed little concern. But as the Cleveland administration knew, the number of treasury notes after 1890 increased while the amount of bullion steadily declined.[22]

President Cleveland made his first official response to the silver problem on June 30, 1893. He reemphasized his widely known anti-Sherman Act position: "The present perilous condition is largely the result of a financial policy which the executive branch of the Government finds embodied in unwise laws which must be executed until repealed by Congress." Therefore it was not surprising when he called for a special session of the House and Senate to remedy the problem. Lawmakers began their deliberations on August 7.[23]

Cleveland won. The congressional battle that subsequently produced silver repeal was intense and often bitter. Inflationists could take only minor satisfaction in knowing that they waged a good fight and that their House champion, William Jennings Bryan of Nebraska, had earned considerable respect for his powers of logic and speech. Although the fear of an inflated currency through the coinage of silver, which Cleveland and others saw as the basic cause of hard times, could now be laid to rest, repeal of the Sherman Act failed to bring relief. Still, the president continued his obsession with a fixed monetary panacea for recovery. This perspective led him to back four separate bond issues designed to replenish the gold reserve and thereby to create business confidence. Also, Cleveland worked closely with the Morgan-Belmont investment banking group to handle one of these loans and "to protect the Treasury against the withdrawal of gold."[24]

The "gold-bug" antics of the Grover Cleveland administration touched off and sustained enormous opposition. Coming mainly from the agricultural West and South, "silverites" believed that rigid adherence to a gold standard meant the continuation of depressed conditions. The principal expression of this popular sentiment appeared in the People's party, launched officially in 1891, and the most successful political organization since the Grand Old Party emerged out of the free-soil agitation in the 1850s. At their highly charged Omaha convention in July 1892, Populists adopted the monetary plank that would give them much of their fame: "We demand free and unlimited coinage of silver and gold at the present legal ratio of 16 to 1."[25]

Although the national ticket of James B. Weaver and James G. Field faltered badly and only a handful of Populists earned seats in the 1893 Congress, the economic collapse attracted more individuals to the silver camp. Even hard-core, "advanced" reformers, who for years pushed tirelessly for the greenback or subtreasury cures for the nation's economic ills, saw the free coinage of silver as a workable short-term expedient against deflation. Commented an Oregon trade unionist in a burst of extreme optimism: "All men of good intent are rallying to the standard of silver." A young Democratic congressman from Virginia, Claude A. Swanson, summed up nicely these widely held inflationist notions in a February 1895 speech on the House floor. "For the last two years every evil, all depression, and stagnation have been ascribed to 'lack of confidence in our currency,'" he reminded his colleagues. "We were told that confidence would be restored and prosperity would return if the purchases of silver under the Sherman Act should cease. The purchases ceased, but prosperity failed to come. We were then told that confidence would not be restored until the President sold bonds and replenished the gold reserves and when this was done business, trade, and commerce would revive." With considerable oratorical skill, Congressman Swanson explained the silverites' version of the Cleveland "lack of confidence" analysis:

> Sirs, the lack of confidence in our country is not in our currency. There is not a dollar of that which is not everywhere sought and desired. The lack of confidence in our country is the lack of confidence that a farmer can raise cotton at 5 cents a pound and pay his debts. The lack of confidence is that the great agricultural classes at the present price for cattle, wheat, corn, and oats cannot pay expenses and discharge their indebtedness. Restore confidence there and all the difficulties which overshadow us will be dissipated. For the solvency of the business and mercantile classes are dependent ultimately upon the farms.

He closed understandably with the silverite refrain: "The country to-day is suffering from a lack of bimetallism. To my mind [the gold standard] can only bring to the country less money, lower prices, great wretchedness and poverty."[26]

While advocates of the free-silver position found the Cleveland administration's rigid adherence to the gold standard unthinkable, the vast majority of Republicans pressed hard to change the president's low-tariff stance. Yet they could not embrace the "heresy of silver." Thus the GOP ideals contained the desire for protectionism together with an orthodox money policy.

Democrats historically favored free trade while Republicans backed tariff barriers to protect manufacturers. The McKinley Tariff of 1890 called for the latter, and the former found expression in the Wilson-Gorman Act of 1894. Indeed, President Cleveland considered lower schedules as a mandate from the electorate of 1892. Most Republicans could accept the logic of Senator John Sherman of Ohio when he blasted the newly passed Wilson measure as "the cause of all the evils we now encounter by adverse balance of trade, by exportation of gold, and derangement of our monetary system." The remedy for depression, rather, must be found in a tariff policy that would "open mills for the full and unrestricted labor of American workingmen." The William McKinley and Republican congressional victories of 1896 quickly led to the implementation of the party's pledge for tariff revision. The Dingley Act, signed July 22, 1897, not surprisingly raised average import duties to record levels.[27]

While the depression years saw persistent wrangling in Washington over how to cope effectively with the troubled economy, the federal political process experienced a variety of demands that did not involve confidence, silver, or the tariff. Easily the most memorable request to Congress came from a Massillon, Ohio, quarry-owner–turned-reformer, Jacob S. Coxey. He initially hoped to create massive employment opportunities with a national road building program to be financed by $500 million in new greenbacks. Subsequently this mild-mannered Ohioan developed a second and longer-lived idea, formulated in early 1894, "The Coxey Non-Interest Bond Bill." Specifically, this proposal called for any state and local governmental unit to make public improvements, presumably labor intensive, by depositing with the national treasury a "non-interest bearing twenty-five year bond, not to exceed one-half of the assessed valuation of the property . . . and said bond to be retired at the rate of four percent per annum."[28]

Together with his future son-in-law, Carl Browne, an ex-carnival barker and labor editor, Jacob Coxey in the spring of 1894 led a march of the jobless to Washington, D.C., "the petition in boots," to seek enactment of the two proposals. The appearance of the main "General Coxey's Army" at the Capitol failed to produce the hoped for legislation. The good-roads bill, introduced by Populist Senator William A. Peffer of Kansas, received no more than an adverse committee report.[29]

Yet the Coxey phenomenon vividly demonstrated both the

depth of depressed conditions and the growing urge to experiment. Ideological rigidities did not inhibit the "General" and his supporters. Coxeyites merely offered a pragmatic solution to a difficult problem. The reform-oriented press repeatedly viewed this particular episode as a popular expression of deep-seated disgust with the national legislative process. "Our legislators are on the wrong track," concluded a Washington state editor, "that hard times are not caused or cured by adherence to gold or the tariff. . . . The money obtained for constructing good roads and public works is a sure winner, if Congress could only be made to see it that way." As one Kansas journalist noted, "At the least Coxey has started many people to thinking who never thought upon economic finance questions before."[30]

Municipal government officials regularly responded to the challenge of hard times, often with a vigor similar to the Coxeyites. After all, they more than lawmakers in a remote capital knew intimately the scope of the economic slide. Local responses usually followed a distinct pattern. Immediately after the panic struck, these public figures, pressured by worried taxpayers, trimmed payrolls to the bone and either postponed or hurriedly completed capital-improvement projects. Such acts of retrenchment naturally exacerbated the negative impact of drastic spending cuts made by the private sector.

Soon a general expression of the validity of Coxey-like pump-priming notions occurred. Throughout the country major municipalities undertook a rich variety of schemes, paid for by the public coffers, to employ the able idle. Boston sponsored wharf improvements, St. Louis underwrote the digging of Forest Park Lake, and Seattle built a central firehouse. Frequently communities intensified their sidewalk and road-repair programs, and street-cleaning activities increased. Of course many local governments lacked the financial wherewithal to support even the most modest public works tasks; bank failures were high and tax collections low.[31]

The saga of state governments' response to the plight of the depressed largely parallels the overall inaction of federal officials. Generally speaking, uncertainty about what options existed for relief and recovery and the low ebb of treasuries explain the limited support for the out-of-work. Still, exceptions occurred. Colorado is one case in point. Not only did the 1893 legislature appropriate funds to help distressed farmers purchase seed grains, but the state's chief executive, Davis H. Waite, backed a novel antidepression device. His scheme, albeit unsuccessful, was the legalization of the Mexican silver dollar. While a clever way of expanding the money supply, the dubious constitutionality of the idea flawed it considerably, although Waite understandably thought it lawful. "As a matter of constitutional law," the governor argued, "there can be no doubt that the concurrent right of the national government to make legal tender does not in any way affect the right of a State to make gold and silver coins, domestic and foreign, a legal tender within its borders."[32]

Aside from those governmental units able and willing to extend helping hands, depression victims initially faced two likely alternatives: individual self-reliance or assistance from private or public charities. The former quite naturally offered limited possibilities, except perhaps for rural residents who had access to food production. Even financially hard-pressed prairie wheat growers probably owned flocks of chickens and swine and a few cattle as well. Plentiful supplies of wild game might exist locally. On the other hand, their city cousins, utterly dependent upon the wage system, lacked this potential for self-sufficiency. Wrote a Buffalo, New York, editor in November 1893, "Many city people are put to their wits' end [during] these hard times to secure the actual necessities of life." He went on to comment that "many of these souls are former farmers and . . . could feed themselves if they had an acreage." Some were able to return temporarily to the farms of relatives or close friends, and there were those who filed for western homesteads, although times were hardly auspicious for launching an agrarian operation from scratch. No matter where their home, all could cut their expenditures. However, excessive thrift became merely a brief stopgap for those with little or no income. As for other workable responses, the *Cleveland Citizen,* tongue-in-cheek, suggested that the unemployed "sleep until noon every day, so that it will be necessary to eat one meal." But the paper seriously urged urban dwellers especially to consume less and to buy such wholesome and cheap food products as that Civil War favorite, rolled oats. Toledo's famed reform mayor, Samuel "Golden Rule" Jones, regularly urged employers to adopt the eight-hour day. "I am doing the best I know how for these people by pleading for the introduction of a shorter day," he told a Chicago social worker, "in order to divide up and give more men work, which seems to me to be the easiest thing that can be done at present."[33]

Reports of bizarre self-help schemes commonly made the front pages of the national press. Frustrated East Colorado wheat farmers, for example, turned to rainmaking. This 1894 effort to end the drought came to naught. "We spent our last money and got no rain," reported participant Fred Jones. Yet this futile, even pathetic, act yielded one benefit: "We had the satisfaction of doing something," adding also the widely held world view that "Being Americans we had a highly developed disposition to do something." And desperate people did desperate things, whether they lived in a farmstead or a tenement. One disturbed Jefferson County, New York, agrarian traded away his wife for a horse, wagon, and harness, while a similarly troubled Philadelphian sold his family, a wife and two children, and their household effects. The sale brought four dollars, but the "man knows that his loved ones will get proper victuals." In the same vein, acts of prostitution increased noticeably. "Shop and factory girls are selling their virtue because of the hard times," announced a Chicago paper. "The poor things must have money to eat and to support their helpless families."[34]

Private charities served as the mainstay for tens of thousands of unfortunate people throughout much of the depression. Such organizations faced enormous demands on their resources of money and personnel. Yet they often responded effectively. While the public sector offered some alms and other assistance, the needy usually could expect better treatment and greater relief options from privately funded agencies. Lacking cumbersome bureaucratic structures, charities could respond quickly. They usually enjoyed immunity from the retrenchment mentality that controlled their public counterparts, and a spirit of innovation permeated their general outlook. Understandably, the desperate conditions forced both public and private groups at times to join forces.

While private charities sponsored the ever-present soup kitchens and bread lines, they also launched such betterment programs as woodyards, relief camps, and industrial farms almost as soon as the economic crunch began. All three stressed the work ethic. Woodyards were places where the able cut fuel for themselves and for the needy who could not handle this manual labor. Also such yards commonly paid workers small cash wages or more likely awarded them meal and lodging tickets that these hungry and frequently homeless individuals could redeem at charity-supported eating halls and dormitories. Relief camps were expanded woodyards. Usually constructed and maintained by the sweat of the unemployed and located in the larger communities, these centers provided food and shelter in return for labor—woodcutting, broom making, or some other cottage industry activity. Like woodyard volunteers, participants in these labor camps might earn cash or scrip. There were only Spartan accommodations—probably tents in warm weather and flimsy barracks during the colder months. Occasionally a local charity might lease or occupy an abandoned factory or warehouse. Industrial farms, pioneered by the Salvation Army, represent a less popular, albeit more comprehensive, approach to assisting the down-and-out. Continuing the concept of an exchange of work for assistance, farms offered more than a service or a few craft occupations; they repeatedly turned to commercial truck, even small-grain farming, and to dairy or cattle and hog raising. Moreover, these settlements, usually located on the outer fringes of urban areas, often provided patrons with educational opportunities and minor health benefits. Indeed, industrial farms strikingly paralleled the utopian intentional communities of the era.[35]

Two ways in which private charities confronted the challenges of the depression were apparent in the activities of Baltimore's Central Relief Committee and the Helping Hand Society of Steubenville, Ohio. In the Maryland metropolis, a practical, no-nonsense spirit guided the leadership of the relief work. A coordinating body consisting of members from a combination of long-established Catholic, Jewish, and Protestant groups speedily came into being during the summer of 1893. Relying on the available financial resources of its supporting organizations, the committee also added to its coffers through a general appeal for contributions. By using an existing outreach center for the poor, "The Friendly Inn," these sensitive Baltimorians were able quickly and effectively to expand the size and scope of their assistance.

The inn fed and housed the poor. But most faced work assignments before eating and sleeping. The Central Relief Committee organized two types of jobs—wood splitting and stone crushing. The former efforts meant fuel for the disadvantaged while the latter provided the raw ingredient for macadamizing roads. The so-called stoneyards, which by the winter of 1893–1894 totaled four, received a much needed boost when city fathers agreed to buy the processed rock. Soon they became the principal source of charity-sponsored employment. To operate them effectively the committee inaugurated a system of payment, usually only scrip for use at the inn. Fifty cents was the price fixed for a unit of work that could be accomplished by a person of ordinary strength in about four hours;

the committee awarded one dollar for double the task. "The feasibility of providing industrial work for relief purposes on a fairly large scale," concluded the *Forum,* "has been successfully demonstrated."[36]

Steubenville, an Ohio River mining and trade center of approximately 14,000 residents, benefited from private charity action. While obviously on a much smaller scale than the Baltimore relief program, the Steubenville story is similar. Spearheaded by the female King's Daughters fraternal society, the town witnessed the formation in early 1894 of a mission designed to feed the hungry and to provide temporary shelter for the homeless. As with Baltimore's Friendly Inn, able-bodied males were asked to work, usually by breaking stove wood, before they could have soup and cots. Steubenville's "Helping Hand Society" functioned also as a clearing house for used garments. During one week in January 1895 it gave out "1134 pieces of clothing, 2 pairs of shoes, 1 pair of mittens, [and] 1 bed comfort." The Helping Hand people also served as an employment bureau. With wall posters and copy provided to the community newspaper, the services of the out-of-work and needy were duly announced. A typical notice ran: "We are prepared to furnish: One woman for quilting; one woman for washing; one woman for housecleaning; one woman for plain sewing; one trusty boy to do errands; one man for re-seating cane-bottomed chairs; one man for painting and papering." The society expected the parties involved to reach their own financial arrangements. By depression's end a Steubenville resident summed up the efforts of the Helping Hand Society with these words: "A Godsend to the people. . . . The suffering would have been worse. The King's Daughters made people feel that they had worth."[37]

THE COMMITMENT TO WORK permeated the national psyche during the depression. "There is something wrong when men who are able and ready to work are compelled to go hungry because they cannot find work to do," observed a midwestern editor in 1895, adding the oft-made comment that *"the opportunity to labor is what is wanted."* He closed with the popular question, "What is the matter with our civilization that such an opportunity is lacking in any civilized and Christian community?"[38]

This great emphasis on toil is thoroughly understandable. Undeniably, the first and foremost quality of the American character was the glorification of the work ethic. From the earliest days of settlement residents recognized that labor was the price of survival in an often hostile frontier environment. Every citizen must be up and doing; one either worked or starved. This spirit is graphically reflected in the 1619 Virginia law that ordered slothful individuals bound over to perform compulsory labor and in the early edict of the Massachusetts Bay Company that "noe idle drone bee permitted to live amongst us." The folk wisdom of the subsequent centuries repeated paeans of praise to the strenuous life. "Work hard and be thrifty," children were warned, "or you'll end up on the poor farm." All were cautioned that time was not always available for niceties. Hours must not be wasted; they were precious: "Life is too short to teach a jack mule to sing soprano." One could look, for example, at the lumber, transportation, and farming frontiers to realize that the leading folk heroes associated with each, Paul Bunyan, Mike Fink, and the myth-embroidered Johnny Appleseed, worked mightily from dawn to dusk.[39]

Historically the emphasis on toil meant more than merely providing for material needs. The public also saw work as a means of spiritual development, almost as a sacrament. Unmistakably, the concept enjoyed Biblical support and commonly highlighted the writings of such notable theologians as St. Augustine and John Calvin. "To work is to pray" served as a vital credo of American religion. Whether church goers or not, probably few truly disagreed with the iconoclastic Elbert Hubbard's assertion that "Work stops bickering, strife and . . . waste. It makes for health and strength."[40]

In the 1890s, however, the nature of work was undergoing a radical change. The traditional society of primitive farms, independent countinghouses, and artisan workshops was giving way to a new one of bonanza agriculture, investment banking, and monstrous smokestack industries with corps of professional managers and armies of workers. Laborers likely realized that technological developments and the routinization and division of labor had left the artisanal structure in shambles. Yet most refused to reject the well-ingrained work ethic, exemplifying nicely cultural persistence amid socioeconomic change. At this particular time the "work or starve" mentality held special significance. And the challenges of the day required a tough response; for most toilers, the national heritage of labor seemed more appropriate than ever.[41]

Not only did Americans believe in the work ethic, they typically lacked hostility towards menial, even dangerous, jobs. The able-bodied craved employment. Few seemed to worry much about the character of the task to be performed; they were not alienated. Coal miners, for example, clamored to be hired for the exceedingly hazardous assignment of dynamiter during these hard times and, even later, operators found no shortage of applicants. As one Indian Territory "shot firer" put it: "I do anything to have eats for the folks." And he had nine mouths to feed.[42]

As might be expected, the charity literature of the era exalted the ethic of work. In February 1894 Josephine S. Lowell, for one, underscored the nearly universally held belief that relief programs might be dangerous. Mrs. Lowell, "a close student of sociological problems [and] one of the foremost practical workers in the relief of distress," worried about individuals who became dependent on the dole. Of course she realized that the country's unfortunate required assitance: "Relief work seems the natural remedy." But Mrs. Lowell made her warning clear.

> [Relief] tempts the industrious, because it is called work and is usually highly paid as compared with regular work, to leave the latter, which is permanent, and to depend upon the relief work, which soon fails them; and it tempts the unstable and the lazy because it is not continuous, and they are allowed to work in a slack and unworkmanlike manner.[43]

Similarly, the unemployed themselves resisted taking help from either private or public charities. "Many sensitive persons will suffer rather than accept charity, even from their relatives and neighbors," noted the 1897 annual report of the New York Charity Organization Society, and this was not an exceptional statement. Whether the depression victims thought the dole would destroy their souls is unclear, but it is known that they firmly accepted the work ethic. Thousands were forced to take aid, since circumstances beyond their control prevented them from doing honest toil for the accustomed income.[44]

This antipathy toward direct aid had deep roots. The literature associated with earlier depressions, particularly the panics of 1837 and 1873, repeatedly contain this theme. President Martin Van Buren in September 1837 argued:

> Those who look to the action of this Government for specific aid to the citizen to relieve embarrassments arising from losses by revulsions in commerce and credit lose sight of the ends for which it was created and the powers with which it is clothed.

> . . . [Government] was established to give security to us all in
> our lawful and honorable pursuits, under the lasting safe-
> guard of republican institutions. It was not intended to confer
> special favors on individuals or on any classes of them. . . .

The *New York Herald* of November 6, 1873, suggested that "all
that we require to bridge over the [hard] times successfully is self-
reliance." But Toledo Mayor Samuel "Golden Rule" Jones in 1897
put it best: "We live with the past that instructs us to work and to
avoid handouts at all cost. In that respect the present panic years
are no different from those of the past."[45]

During the depression individuals of good will, particularly
members of the emerging social settlement-house and social gospel
movements, made numerous efforts to assist the down-and-out.
While they employed or encouraged with some caution soup kitchens and used clothing and fuel centers, they also created new programs, the leading one being the public garden. Still, the desire to
reinforce the virtues of work and to avoid the direct handout nearly
always characterized their own efforts.

An important source of comfort and hope for America's disadvantaged were innovative self-help plans. The story of five of
these bootstrap schemes reveals much more than the contemporary
perception that without work the country would surely lose its soul.
For contained in community gardens, labor exchanges, cooperative
stores, farmers' railroads, and intentional colonies are two central
elements. The more obvious and important is the desire for *immediate* relief from the ravages of hard times. The other is a craving
for *permanent* solutions to suffering, a theme intimately tied to the
idea of reform. Unquestionably these dual objectives dominate the
thought and action of a concerned populace during the disaster of
1893 to 1897.

# Community Gardens

OMMUNITY GARDENS flourished as the most widely adopted and supported self-help concept during the depression of the 1890s. Thus they are the most significant of the pragmatic solutions Americans developed when faced with unemployment and the specter of starvation. While these plots were not generally viewed as panaceas for the evils of unemployment, *Charities Review* correctly characterized them as "the [most] useful emergency measure to help those who are temporarily out of work to support life . . . by honorable toil." Since gardens worked so well, the notion persisted; gardens regularly appeared during subsequent economic dislocations and periods of national emergencies.[1]

Detroit, Michigan, was the birthplace of the modern community garden. The depression of the nineties ravaged this metropolis of slightly more than 200,000 people. During the early months of hard times workers generally had their wages cut, but soon many faced more troublesome problems. The city's leading employers, including the Detroit Stove Works, the Michigan-Peninsular Car Company, and the Pullman Company, either suspended or drastically slashed production. By 1894 about 25,000 of approximately 75,000 workers knew idleness. The foreign born were especially hard hit; German and Polish laborers flooded the pauper rolls. Local benevolent organizations tried to help, but like those elsewhere found themselves increasingly unable to cope with the swelling numbers of unemployed. Fortunately for both Detroit and the nation, the incumbent mayor, Hazen Stuart Pingree, not only was sensitive to human suffering, but devised the immensely popular and effective response that soon bore his name, "Pingree's Potato Patch."[2]

Who was Hazen Pingree—a man contemporary admirers called a "Moses of the masses?" Born near Denmark, Maine, on August 30, 1840, the son of an impoverished farmer and sometimes cobbler, Pingree grew up with adversity. At fourteen he left school for the drudgery of a cotton mill, and later he toiled in a leather factory. When the Civil War broke out, young Pingree rallied to the colors by joining the First Massachusetts Heavy Artillery. He not only experienced the horrors of war at the Second Battle of Bull Run and the Battle of North Anna River in Virginia, but spent five torturous months during 1864 in the infamous Confederate prison camp at Andersonville, Georgia.[3]

While Hazen Pingree's early years were difficult, the latter part of his life became the stuff that made the Horatio Alger rags to riches stories seem so plausible. Pingree arrived in Detroit at war's end with little money, but with hard work, brilliance, and luck, his new career as a boot and shoe manufacturer made him a wealthy man within a relatively short time.[4]

In 1889 Pingree the successful businessman became Pingree the successful politician. In that year voters overwhelmingly elected him mayor of Detroit on the Republican ticket, a position he would hold until 1897. Initially, he viewed himself as a good-government candidate, and consequently he enjoyed the support of the community's business elite. Indeed, local capitalists urged him to seek elective office. But Pingree was not content to remain a "goo-goo," for he perceived the city to be suffering from problems that would not be solved solely by installing civic uplifters in office. By the time depression struck, Pingree had formed a powerful political organization based on a coalition of workers and ethnics rather than the "better people," many of whom believed that the mayor had "joined the mob." Further angering the patricians, Pingree turned enthusiastically to a broad-gauged program of consumerism. His efforts to protect the public interest included a strenuous fight against the street-traction firms and an equally zealous crusade for municipal ownership of electric lighting. By the mid-1890s Hazen Pingree personally had done much to make Detroit a center of emerging urban progressivism.[5]

While he envisioned a better world based on the tenets of "gas and water" socialism, Pingree realized that change, at best, occurred slowly. Yet the urgent needs of Detroit's poor demanded immediate action; residents were hungry, even starving. The mayor's solution to this problem was amazingly simple: he started community gardens. In early 1894, Pingree launched this stop-gap relief

*Mayor Hazen S. Pingree, creator of the modern community garden movement (second from right) and Captain Cornelius Gardener (left), chairman of the Agricultural Committee, inspect a Detroit self-help garden in 1894.*

program, which the local populace immediately dubbed "the Detroit Plan," "the Agricultural Scheme," or more commonly "Pingree's Potato Patch."

The exact origins of the garden concept remain clouded. Perhaps the mayor merely recalled his Maine boyhood. Although the Pingree household regularly faced cash shortages, the family seemed to have ample foodstuffs, including plenty of potatoes and turnips. An associate remarked that the idea "occurred to Mr. Pingree, while driving along the Boulevard in Detroit, that could but the poor and unemployed get a chance to cultivate some of the vacant and idle lands there [they could survive]." An unpublished biography of Pingree written by Cyril and Marjorie Player in 1931 suggests that "There is substantial living evidence . . . that the project originated in the gentle, anxious mind of Mrs. Pingree." The Players speculate that the mayor's wife may have either seen or heard of the English "allotment plans," where the poor, through a system of rents, enjoyed access to garden plots. There exists still another explanation. A Pingree friend, Capt. Cornelius Gardener, stationed at Detroit's historic Fort Wayne with the Nineteenth U.S. Infantry, apparently was well acquainted with the value of gardens at military posts. Pingree himself noted that the affable Captain "was the first person with whom I conversed in relation to cultivating the waste land in the suburbs of the city." Captain Gardener's role in the formulation of the potato-patch scheme is unmistakable; he subsequently served as chairman of the Detroit Agricultural Committee that supervised the gardens.[6]

Regardless of the etiology of the potato patches, Mayor Pingree turned his attention to self-help on June 6, 1894. He told the press of his intention to seek vacant lots to feed the needy. The next day he asked local ministers to assist him on Sunday in publicizing the plan and in the all-important function of raising funds to acquire seeds and tools. Pingree appealed to the clergy's sense of Christian service: "The destitution of many of the inhabitants of Detroit is well known, and the outlook for them the coming winter to procure food to keep body and soul together is gloomy in the extreme." The ministers' weak response stunned the Mayor. Although they probably mentioned the plan, their seemingly uncaring attitude, reflective, too, of the city's elite, saw that Sunday's special offering netting a paltry $13.80.[7]

Undaunted, Hazen Pingree turned to a proven political technique and one of his trademarks—publicity. He announced with great fanfare his intention to offer at public auction his prized brood mare, "Josie Wilkes," to raise money for the gardens. He also told of his plans to sell tickets for a circus to be held on the grounds of the Detroit Athletic Club to aid the potato-patch idea. Pingree, moreover, informed the citizenry that he personally would assist in the planting, weeding, and harvesting and that the elegant lawn of his upper Woodward Avenue mansion could be used for "practical charity." These newsworthy comments further aided advertising and subsequently brought donations of land and money. Clearly the mayor successfully evoked a sense of urgency, excitement, pride in activism, and experimentation.[8]

The administrative framework of the potato patches was thoroughly practical. The Common Council created a quasi-public, seven-member volunteer agricultural committee to supervise the project. Applications for garden space came either directly to the committee or more often through the preexisting City Poor Commission. The land itself was donated by individuals and corporations. (The assessor's office provided information on vacant lots, the majority of which clustered on Detroit's outer fringe where depression halted most development.) Once real estate had been obtained, the agricultural committee oversaw the plowing, harrowing, and the staking off of plots. Initially the units contained an acre, but subsequently they were reduced to one-quarter to one-half acre when more than three thousand families applied. Even then, less than one-third of the seekers received land. After making garden assignments—officials tried to find space near the applicant's home—the committee furnished seed potatoes, cabbage plants,

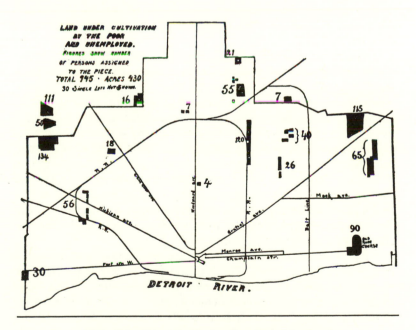

Map of the "potato patches" under cultivation in 1894. During the first year nearly 1,000 Detroit families tilled more than 400 acres of idle land.

beans, turnips, and other seeds. Necessary hand tools were likewise provided. A salaried foreman supervised planting, although many participants had previous gardening experience as ex-farmers from Europe. Experts from the local D. M. Ferry Seed Company, the Michigan Agricultural College at East Lansing, and the engineering staff of the Detroit Water Board also assisted.[9]

The agricultural committee encountered potentially serious problems during its formative days. Under pressure to start, the committee discovered it was virtually impossible to eliminate those parcels with poor-quality soil. The actual gardening did not begin until late in the growing season, and a nine-week drought delayed or prevented some plantings. Yet the first year proved to be amazingly successful. On approximately 430 acres, 945 financially troubled Detroit families produced crops conservatively valued at $14,000. The committee's expenses, paid mostly from donated funds, amounted to only $3,632. Not only did the gardens produce more than 40,000 bushels of potatoes, but the bean crop was bountiful. Furthermore as Captain Gardener noted, "the squashes and pumpkins planted did exceedingly well, and in some cases gave enormous yields."[10]

The potato patches themselves were memorable sights. "Far as the eye can reach they spread, uneven, diversified, and incongruous," observed the Detroit *Evening News*. "There are no fences to obstruct the view, just one great big, nodding, smiling potato patch, stretched out beneath the red, inquisitive eye of the August sun." The gardens surely held special meaning for the participants. The growing crops naturally meant food, both for the long winter months ahead and for immediate consumption. "Many families from dire want," reported the agricultural committee, "were obliged to dig up for consumption portions of their potatoes before they had attained any size." Since there were no restrictions on how crops could be used, some families successfully peddled their surplus vegetables for precious income.[11]

Dividends, however, exceeded the nutritional and monetary value of the truck goods. Tending the plots made for a pleasant outing. Even though gardening was not heavy work, it was labor intensive. Entire families frequently came to the fields where they chatted amongst themselves and gossiped with neighboring tillers, often in their native tongues. (This camaraderie may explain the overall absence of crop vandalism and thievery.) The potato patches, moreover, brought people out-of-doors, away from crowded tenements, into the healthful air. A trip to the garden surely helped to break the monotony of the workers' dull and dreary existence. And there was the excitement associated with meeting the beloved mayor, who repeatedly visited these scattered sites. Finally, one notable benefit was the sense of pride, not only in raising crops, but in avoiding the food dole.[12]

Hazen Pingree and the residents of Detroit showed no desire to abandon the potato patches. Typical of the letters of support was this one: "We are Penniless with nothing Put in for the Winter. If we could have the Potatoes, we would thankfully return the same in the Fall." Local poets, too, expressed approval. One penned the following piece:

> Here we are, and fun await us!
> Spread your mouth and contemplate us;
> Hurrah for Pingree and potatoes,
> Whoop ta ra ra boom de ay!
>
> Away with all your sour grimaces;
> Away with all your long drawn faces;
> Take them off to other places;
> Whoop ta ra ra boom de ay!
>
> Give all the poor a holiday!
> Give all the town a jolly day;
> What does Tom and Molly say?
> Whoop ta ra ra boom de ay!
>
> There's not a cent in melancholy,
> To hang your lip in rankest folly;
> Let's help the poor by being jolly!
> Whoop ta ra ra boom de ay!
>
> Here we are and fun await us!
> Spread your mouth and contemplate us;
> Hurrah for Pingree and potatoes,
> Whoop ta ra ra boom de ay!

While some political adversaries mocked the mayor by calling him "Tuber I," they knew that the plots worked and worked well. An underlying consideration was the conservative elite's nearly universal fear of mob rule. Before the gardens, ominous cries of "Bread or blood!" had been heard on Detroit streets. But with the Pingree scheme, conditions dramatically improved. Observed one merchant, "Full stomachs have an amazingly calming effect on people." Few disagreed.[13]

The 1895 season saw even more of Detroit's unemployed gardening. That year there were 1,546 families, as depressed conditions continued and more donated land became available. The patches blossomed. More than twice the value of the inaugural year's goods was produced. "Almost every variety of vegetable was raised but mainly potatoes, beans and turnips," recounted the agricultural committee.[14]

The Detroit Plan was strengthened and refined. Of major significance, the common council assumed full control of gardening. It appropriated $5,000, thus eliminating the "pass-the-hat" funding of the first year. The committee reserved forty-eight lots in which it directed the planting of potatoes and turnips to replace crops lost to cultivators when donated land was sold for development. This year the program could meet all the needs of applicants, so the committee even rented a few plots to those individuals who, though not destitute, wanted to garden. In order to maintain and to improve crop production, Pingree and the committee ordered manure, so plentiful in the age of animal traffic, deposited on the various plots by street cleaners before and after the growing season.[15]

Levels of participation and performance similar to 1894 and 1895 continued for the next two years, the final period of depression. Not surprising, 1898 saw a significant decline in the scope of the potato patches. As that year's annual report of the agricultural committee noted, "The falling off of the number of applicants for lots . . . is largely attributable to the return of more prosperous times." Still, 994 families gardened. This degree of involvement continued through 1901, when the city terminated the program.[16]

Before the Detroit Plan ended, the committee attempted to solve a major weakness and even to institutionalize the scheme. Since the program depended upon free-will donations of planting space and was therefore vulnerable to changes in land usage, the committee recommended that the city purchase at least two hundred acres on either side of Woodward Avenue, the principal division street. In a highly pragmatic fashion it argued that "these farms can, as the city becomes larger, be converted into parks," with the assumption that public land could become instant potato patches if economic disaster should again strike. Mayor Pingree's move to the governor's chair in 1897, and the advent of a healthier economy probably prevented adoption of this plan for municipally owned garden property.[17]

THE STUNNING SUCCESS of Hazen Pingree's community gardens triggered their immediate and widespread imitation. Hundreds of interested individuals wrote the mayor; some even travelled to Detroit for first-hand information. And the national press closely followed the happenings. As early as May 1895, the *New York World* observed that "to-day the name 'Pingree Potato Patch' is known from ocean to ocean. . . . " By the end of the depression, scores of communities offered blooming gardens as their major self-help program. The largest ones naturally appeared in the leading metropolitan centers: Boston, New York, Brooklyn, Buffalo, Philadelphia, Pittsburgh, Chicago, St. Louis, Omaha, Denver, and Seattle. But smaller communities also boasted potato patches. For example, Reading, Pennsylvania; Steubenville, Ohio; Galesburg, Illinois; and Winona, Minnesota adopted the plan.[18]

Likewise confronted with hard times, Europeans resorted to potato patches. Some cases of borrowing occurred, in much the same way as contemporary Americans copied the Swiss initiative and referendum, or German municipal zoning codes, or the Russian subtreasury idea. For the Detroit plan was known shortly "even in some of the effete municipalities of Europe." Unemployed distillery workers of Delft, Holland, for example, got idle land from their employer and "followed the Americans." Of course the concept of public garden space was firmly established in several Old World countries before the economic slide of the 1890s and would continue to flourish widely in the twentieth century. The time-honored English "allotment plan," which as already seen conceivably served as the model for Pingree's experiment, is a leading illustration. While remarkably similar to the Detroit affair, British landowners (they might also be municipalities) universally asked participants to pay, albeit nominal, annual rents. Furthermore, these gardens tended to be durable. When depressed conditions disappeared, people commonly cultivated for pleasure rather than for nourishment.[19]

The various American garden programs did not always replicate the Detroit format. For one thing, the types of sponsorship and management varied. Buffalo and Reading, to use prominent examples, relied on public administration. The city treasury paid the entire cost of cultivating, and elected officials provided supervision. (Detroit did not adopt this system until the second year.) The majority of communities utilized existing charitable societies to organize and direct the patches. Examples include Boston, New York,

Brooklyn, Chicago, and Seattle. In Gotham, for instance, a fifty-three-year-old private philanthropic society, the Association for Improving the Condition of the Poor (AICP), operated that city's successful and innovative gardening program. A third organizational form appeared: the independent committee or association created solely for community gardening. Philadelphia, Minneapolis, and Denver opted for this structure. In the "Queen City of the West," for example, a quasi-public consortium operated a sizable vacant-lot project. Launched in 1895, this group consisted of representatives from the Denver Woman's Club, Associated Charities, and city government.[20]

Major modifications to the prototype model likewise occurred. Two prominent illustrations are found in the Empire state—Rochester and New York City. Resembling so many other communities, Rochester began its garden cultivation in 1895. Through the Office of the Overseer of the Poor, the city rented suburban plots for garden space. Rather than allowing the poor to raise their own produce, selected needy persons became municipal employees, producing potatoes for public distribution to the indigent. This plan, unfortunately, was badly flawed. Work was not steady; only about two days' labor was given weekly to each participant. Even though earnings averaged a respectable $3.50 per week, gardeners were not paid in cash but received provisions and fuel from the "Poor Store." Moreover, they lacked a strong personal interest in the plots. Tilling became merely a part-time job, not a labor of love. And the overall scope was severely limited; the public treasury contained only minimal funds for extra aid to the unemployed. Unquestionably, many more families could have benefited if Rochester had followed the Detroit approach.[21]

A much more satisfactory variation to the Pingree plan took place in New York City. In conjunction with extensive Detroit-like potato patches, a cooperative gardening program was also developed. Clearly the sponsor, the AICP, sought to offer more comprehensive self-help assistance.

The AICP began a cooperative farm in 1895, shortly after it launched its 300 acres of potato patches. The site for both schemes was Long Island City, on land obtained principally from manufacturer William Steinway and the Long Island Improvement Company. The AICP conceived the idea of hiring the unemployed to garden at the rate of seven and one-half cents per hour for the first month and then ten cents thereafter with the promise of a share in the annual profits. Anyone hired was likewise eligible to work a regular garden plot. More than a score of able-bodied unemployed enrolled. "Most . . . were men who had once occupied good positions, but through force of circumstances had gotten among the rocks, did not know how to extricate themselves, and took hold of this as a new hope."[22]

The cooperative farm's initial year was successful. The AICP sold the produce to various New York City area charities at the going market prices. This yielded $1,067.65. On the other hand, wages amounted to $966.75; after deducting other expenses (land rentals, costs of superintendance and supplies), $53.00 remained to be divided among the workers. Although paralleling the Rochester program, the AICP scheme enjoyed obvious advantages. The Long Island participants realized more financial benefits because of higher weekly wages, and they shared in the final net profits. Unlike Rochester, these employees also operated their own gardens as part of the AICP's correspondent vacant-lot program. They thus had access to both cash and food. Understandably, the AICP's executive committee relished the cooperative farm notion. In a report issued in early 1895, it concluded that this system of gardening "should be made the main one, as it stimulated the men to friendly rivalry, created a public spirit against loafing, and while affording immediate wages to the cultivators, can be made to contribute largely toward the other expenses of the committee."[23]

WHEN A REPORTER from the *New York World* interviewed a cooperative farm participant, he heard a point-of-view regularly associated with the community garden movement:

> There is no reason why people with minds and strength should not have plenty and to spare, provided they will go [to] the farm and work. There are thousands of men and women in this city to-day who are on the verge of starvation. They will never do as well in a crowded city as they will out on little farms.[24]

This statement contains the essence of an overly simplistic argument that favored community gardens as a device to alter dramatically the nature of the national society—namely, to urge trapped urban dwellers to return to the land. Just as some Americans in the 1930s were to dream of subsistence farming as a practical alternative to depression and the shortcomings of capitalism and as a means to realize a simpler set of values and way of life, this earlier cry seems to have had similar objectives.

The quest for an agrarian utopia of hardy and virtuous yeomen was manifested in more than the desire for garden plots or "little farms." As a writer for the Seattle *Intelligencer* argued, the various potato patches would "create a taste for gardening" that might then be expressed in larger and possibly permanent farming operations. Specifically, plans emerged during the depression of the 1890s for the introduction of thousands of poor and unemployed into Arcadian settings that would both provide relief and "stop the dangerous concentrating tendencies which have so steadily and rapidly increased the proportion of urban population . . . during the past fifty years."[25]

Perhaps the most widely publicized suggestion for back-to-the-land came from the National Irrigation Congress. Headquartered in Great Bend, Kansas, this group of mostly plains agrarians anxiously awaited the "irrigation age," when the Western desert "will bloom to the contentment of those who till." But during the hard times of the nineties the congress saw its role to be more than boosting "underground rain." E. R. Moses, the body's chairman, outlined the possibilities and advantages of what he termed "colossal Potato patches":

> The western half of the U.S. is the only out let for home seekers. There are millions of acres of land that can be used for this purpose by intense cultivation with artificial water. On even 5, 10, 20, or 40 acres of land, a family can make a living and more. This land can be bought cheap. . . .
> This is a sure and profitable investment. It helps people to help themselves and it makes better citizens. The investor is doing a humane act and in the end, is paid for his efforts in and around the cities. One million of people must go back to farming and become producers.[26]

There is little evidence to indicate any significant patterns of urban to rural migration during the depression. Even though the possibilities of irrigation made western real estate seemingly attractive, the dismal state of the economy limited the practical application of the Moses plan. Even so, it may have had a forceful impact. Just as the frontier conceivably acted earlier as a "safety-valve" for discontented urbanites, the notion of a subsistence or small commercial western farm may have produced a similar effect. Indeed, the idea might have been a "psychological safety-valve": individuals may have felt better and thus more able to cope with the realities of the day. Even though never seriously intending to uproot themselves, the economically troubled knew that if conditions worsened, they could always employ this remedy. "Mr. Moses is correct with his notions on how to aid the down and out on a lasting basis," wrote a Wisconsin admirer, "and even if you don't go to eastern Col. or western Kan. you will always feel better with the certain Knowledge that this is a reasonable way out if the Grim Reaper is about to come through the door."[27]

While the Arcadian concept can be linked legitimately to the community garden, an undeniably radical one, the single tax, is likewise associated with it. For in an era before the fusion of most uplifters into the Progressive movement, single-issue groups (vice crusaders, civil service proponents, soft-money advocates, and the like) dominated the national reform scene. Followers of Henry George (1839–1897), the single-tax prophet, represent this type of articulate and dedicated breed. In his famed 1879 work, *Progress and Poverty,* George found the private ownership of land the cause of increasing want. As the plausible remedy, he advocated his much debated tax change: a levy to take away from the landlord for the benefit of the greater society the increase in the value of real estate that was created through no effort of its owner, but which occurred through the toil of the general populace.[28]

Single taxers adored community gardens. While personally concerned about depression victims, they immediately saw the plots as practical demonstrations of the merits of their pet socioeconomic reform, just as they expected the movement's well-known colony at Fairhope, Alabama, started in 1894, to enlighten the citizenry. Soon after Detroit embarked on its potato patches, a local single-tax advocate wrote Mayor Pingree to applaud this novel program: "In your 'potato patch' experiment you have established a precedent, and initiated a custom which, if properly followed up, may prove the beginning of a vastly beneficial modification of the existing system of land tenures." This Georgist viewed gardens as graphically demonstrating "the economic folly and crime of allowing hungry men to stand in enforced idleness on fertile uncultivated land." Ideally, he wanted the national adoption of the single-tax philosophy, but he was willing to settle for public ownership of garden tracts.[29]

In several localities single taxers pushed hard for the Detroit

Plan. One example was Wilmington, Delaware. Early in 1896 a union of the Associated Charities and the Single-Tax Club launched a short-term garden program. These George supporters had the two objectives that characterized single-tax thought and strategy: "The first is to benefit the po[o]r of the city. The second, . . . the more important, is to demonstrate that the thing to solve the labor problem is to give the people free access to the soil, where they can create value, and then there will be none dependent upon the charities."[30]

The premier illustration of the single-tax crusade uniting with the potato-patch movement occurred in Philadelphia. Resembling the Wilmington experience, the Vacant Lots Cultivation Association, started in 1897, attracted not only the principal local charity but die-hard Georgists, including soap czar Joseph Fels. To the followers of Henry George, adoption of the Pingree plan offered a splendid opportunity to show tangibly how economic distress might be easily and permanently removed. After all, these experiments captured the public fancy, and the press regularly chronicled their happenings.[31]

But the hoped-for results of the Philadelphia single-taxers were largely unrealized. Even though ninety-six families, gardening on twenty-seven acres, enjoyed a successful season, the single-tax cause gained few adherents. Nevertheless, proponents likely saw the gardens as positive demonstrations of the truth of the George doctrine. The experience simply reinforced their single-tax beliefs. Mary Fels described her husband's feeling:

> The experiment with the city lots had shown that there was a real hunger for the land; the society from the start had always more applicants than it could supply. Meantime there was no dearth of land. There was no scarcity even of unused land. There was almost a plethora of land deliberately withheld from cultivation or from other improvements, merely for purposes of speculation.[32]

While neither nostalgic nor particularly forward looking, considerable discussion took place during the depression years on whether or not to have community gardens become a permanent feature of the public's overall program for assisting the disadvantaged. Professor E. R. L. Gould of the University of Chicago, who favored the concept, put it best: "I think indeed that such a scheme is applicable to that class of persons whom we know as chronic charity subjects, those always more willing to receive relief than to work." This "workfare" rather than welfare both then and in the future seemed wholly appropriate. "Gardening is not heavy work," he argued, "and all except the physically disabled should welcome such an opportunity to justify the belief that they are worthy of social help."[33]

Although hardly a revolutionary thought, gardening as a prerequisite to the dole never developed much beyond the idea stage during the 1890s. A few charities, however, attempted to use moral suasion to have patrons plant potato patches before they extended a helping hand. Eventually this "garden first" doctrine emerged as a mandatory part of a variety of state public assistance programs during the depression years of the 1930s.


WHILE THE COMMUNITY GARDEN episode failed to serve as a vehicle for either the attainment of the Arcadian ideal or the single tax or even as a means of altering charitable aid, the concept was a practical success as an emergency stopgap measure during the hard times. The plan admittedly was not a cure-all for America's ills. Unquestionably, the editor of the Missouri Valley, Iowa, *Eye* erred when he contended, "Give idle people access to idle lands and hard times will be a thing of the past." Mayor Pingree, for one, would surely have challenged the Hawkeye journalist. A few advanced reformers, who hailed from Populist ranks, thought the plan smacked of paternalism. They wanted "not to confuse Pingree's patches with honest-to-gosh change," although "we think idle labor of the city should garden." Still, unbridled enthusiasm is understandable. Low in cost, easy and swift to implement, and providing substantial economic and human benefits, potato patches boasted all the necessary characteristics of a nearly flawless scheme for immediate need. Inherently unsolvable weaknesses did not haunt it. Those that existed might prove troublesome, but they usually could be handled after a season or two.[34]

The several shortcomings of community gardens appeared immediately. The most common complaint was location. Often the needy lived considerable distances from available plots of ground. After all, the poor generally inhabited the older, decaying parts of cities, squeezed into the original "walking city," where streets were narrow, lot sizes tiny, and dwellings hugged the curbs. With the rapid growth of streetcar, steam car, and even steamboat suburbs after the Civil War, undeveloped land parcels existed in large num-

*Polish-American gardeners who participated in
the Detroit Plan (1894).*

bers only on the urban periphery. Potential cultivators therefore
faced expensive transit fares or long walks.

The potato-patch proponents typically pressed hard for the
right to utilize vacant inner-city space: wasted lands adjoining railroad lines, unused portions of cemeteries, and even the available
lawns. Such property often was obtainable. Most owners recognized the merits of such requests. Not only did gardens keep down
obnoxious weeds but as the Savannah, Georgia, *News* observed,
"The cultivation does not hurt the land and the benefits arising to
those to whom the privilege is granted are considerable." For those
enthusiasts who sought to institutionalize this self-help concept (as
seen in the case of Detroit), public acquisition of real estate in areas
of sizable concentrations of working-class residents seemed the
practical solution—land that could be used during prosperous

times for parks and recreation and then, as needed, converted into gardens.[35]

Coinciding with spatial problems, another one existed with soil quality. Certain communities, of course, never faced this concern, but some did. Chicago is an example. The *Tribune* noted in 1895, the inaugural year for Windy City potato patches, that "while there is plenty of fertile soil about the city, the ground seems to be very poor in the districts where those live whom it is desired to help." Specifically, available land on the North Side was too sandy while South Side lots were too low, repeatedly plagued by standing water, and prone to full-scale flooding.[36]

The poor land bugaboo had solutions. Community garden organizers often were able to improve soil quality. Detroit, as seen earlier, embarked on a systematic program of placing animal manure on the plots. Inexpensive drainage improvements also occurred, but most communities could not afford massive public works efforts of this type. The best answer was to find real estate that needed little, if any, upgrading.

If suitable land—located in desirable places and satisfactory in quality—became community potato patches, still another problem might develop. Namely, plots might be sold during the growing months. Nationally this did not happen often, although incidents of it occurring increased as commercial and residential expansion resumed as hard times waned. Changes in land usage badly disrupted some patches. For instance, Des Moines in 1896 saw several large garden areas, tilled by scores of families, sold and immediately destroyed by road and house construction crews. Paralleling the desire to find appropriate locations, the community garden faithful sought public property that would forever protect the program, or, as in Detroit, wanted auxiliary plots to compensate those who lost the rewards of their labors.[37]

Assuming that cultivators faced no difficulties with the garden space itself, several additional snags might occur. Some participants consumed their food before it had a chance to mature. And in several instances, a crop might never be put in at all; people were too hungry. One illustration is the 1895 Detroit Plan in Kingston, New York, where the "poor ate the seed potatoes, instead of planting them." Also, crop failures occasionally occurred. The problem of proper storage facilities likewise prompted concern. A spokesman for the Kansas City garden efforts observed that "too many of the poor have no place to store vegetables after they have raised them." No single solution was devised. Some movement figures suggested construction of publicly owned warehouse buildings, caves, or root cellars. Some private institutions, usually churches, offered cultivators space in their basements or sheds.[38]

Praise for the Detroit Plan seemed universal. Remarked the standpat Brockton, Massachusetts, *Times,* "Pingree's scheme is practicable and useful." Another expression came from the pen of the editor of the *Saturday Review,* who exclaimed, "Just think of it! A chance for everybody who is out of work to earn a living all summer and save up enough to last through the winter. Not one cent of capital needed, and no 'previous experience' either." These conclusions succinctly caught the national sentiment. The community garden concept was as American as Benjamin Franklin's "Poor Richard" aphorisms. Even if it were not, the fact that the country was a land of desperate people made the public on a cross-class basis view potato patches as thoroughly acceptable. "A few months ago, if any publication had demanded for the masses an opportunity to help themselves, the burning brand of 'socialist' would have consigned it to the wastebasket unnoticed." (This Pennsylvania editor obviously failed to perceive the essence of the experiment, but he correctly recognized its popularity.)[39]

While the community garden approach may be rightly considered as a depression Band-Aid, it offered what reform journalist B. O. Flower called a "valuable palliative measure to supplant the old method of conventional charity which has proved so inefficient, and which has frequently lowered manhood and proved otherwise vicious in its effect on the recipient." Or as the *Los Angeles Times* said, "The true way [gardens] to help the poor is to aid them to help themselves, so that they may maintain their self-respect." The Pingree scheme, moreover, claimed dimensions of both Arcadianism and tax radicalism. But community gardens were, in the words of one commentator, "not enough to complete the required bridge from adversity to prosperity." Therefore, additional self-help notions emerged. They likewise included the limited objective of providing uplift during hard times. Yet they also contained elements designed to change fundamentally American life.[40]

# *Labor Exchange*

A L T H O U G H  community gardens became the best known and the most widely adopted emergency measures during the hard times of the 1890s, kindred plans emerged. A leading illustration of "self-helpers" who wanted to do more than provide for immediate needs were the advocates of the "labor exchange." These people of good hope knew that their idea was not only an instant cure for unemployment, but that it could also restructure the national economic system to make it depression proof and more humane. Labor exchangers realized that their blueprint for a better America, like those ubiquitous potato patches, nicely fit a public mind-set that revered the work ethic and reaffirmed basic American values. "There is no communism, nor anarchy in this," proclaimed one exchange tract.[1]

Resembling most popular reform and self-help notions during the depression, the labor exchange scheme predated the industrial collapse. Actually, it traced its origins back to the 1870s when one thoughtful midwesterner desired to help the financially troubled. Much of the early history of the labor exchange is thus the story of its founder, G. B. De Bernardi.

Although calling himself a "Missouri farmer," Giovanni Battista De Bernardi was hardly typical of fellow "show-me" state agrarians. Unlike neighbors in highly Anglo Jackson County (Kansas City and Independence), he hailed from Italy, specifically from the Alpine community of Zubiena, Piedmont. De Bernardi's training, too, was unusual. Born into an upper-class family on February 2, 1831, he was given a solid private education, inspired largely by an interested uncle who headed a respected local school. Bright and intellectually curious, De Bernardi subsequently continued his studies in Paris. While in the French capital he became fascinated with political and economic matters. After three years De Bernardi drifted to England to pursue his interests in political economy. Then, while listening to an Italian musician in a Liverpool cafe sing of America, according to one account, he decided to "study for himself the institutions of the free."[2]

G. B. De Bernardi arrived in the United States in 1858. He travelled to the Missouri frontier, acquired a small farm near the famed Santa Fe Trail community of Independence, and married a local girl. Involved with his home and family, De Bernardi failed to grapple with either political or economic issues until the economy worsened following the "Panic of '73." Then he revived his former interests.[3]

Infected with Grangerism, the widespread contemporary movement of the Patrons of Husbandry that sought both political reform and self-help, De Bernardi urged residents not only to support Granger candidates but to utilize a consumer-owned store to buy supplies and market products. Because of inadequate financial backing, the plan accomplished little. Although details of De Bernardi's activities prior to 1890 are tantalizingly obscure, it is known that he tried to launch still another cooperative store in the mid-eighties. Again, he produced minimal results, although he likely gained practical experience in the nature of such enterprises.[4]

In 1890, convinced that he had something of importance to say about the problems of the industrial age, G. B. De Bernardi penned a 262-page tract, *Trials and Triumph of Labor*.[5] This basis for the labor exchange placed De Bernardi squarely in the mainstream of those who sought to end unemployment by increasing the amount of circulating medium. He welcomed greenbacks, free coinage of silver, or any other inflationary device. But he differed from most currency reformers in that he foresaw the "soft money" objective as probably unobtainable because of the fickle nature of the political process. "This ballot box method is about as practical as Bellamy's plan of sleeping it out." De Bernardi also turned his attention away from the farmer toward the urban worker. Possibly he felt that the agrarians as a class were doomed. At one point he noted as much in his book: "Many of our farmers have recently been forced off their lands by the relentless suction of the devouring mortgage and are now part of the poorly paid and exploited working class. [Workers] more than any group need my help."[6]

G. B. De Bernardi saw the need for immediate relief as well as for long-lasting reform. Rather than waiting until uplifters captured the Capitol and the White House, he hoped to establish cooperative, grass-roots organizations that would enable the poor to at least acquire the necessities of life. "The hungry unemployed want relief now," he argued, "and can not wait for the slow and uncertain movements of the law." But De Bernardi had no desire to create a merely ephemeral program. What he longed for was an economic system that might eventually replace, or at least be grafted onto, capitalism. Minimally, his proposal could continue to function and easily expand during a future "bust."[7]

De Bernardi launched the labor exchange in late 1889, several months before the official publication of his first book. Rather than selecting his home community, Independence, he chose Sedalia, Missouri, a neighboring railroad town with high unemployment, a penchant for radicalism, and a milieu seemingly conducive to experimentation. A year later, he had the state officially incorporate the exchange.[8]

The structure of the De Bernardi scheme was simple. A nucleus of fifteen to twenty persons (males and females) would establish a branch at the cash cost to each participant of one dollar for a life membership. This would be the only required outlay of money since he believed that the old Grange system of cash-only cooperatives, based on the English Rochdale plan (see Chap. Three), made little sense during hard times, and that stores sponsored by the Farmers' Alliance—that precursor to Populism—suffered similar

The Akron, Ohio, Labor Exchange local distributed this business card ca. 1900.

weaknesses. He emphasized that "While the Rochdale and Alliance enter the economic field by way of commerce, we enter it at the gates of production. While their object is to bear down prices that money may reach further into products, our object is to create abundance that all may fare bountifully."[9]

Upon the granting of a charter, the labor exchange local would elect officers and organize a warehouse financed from individual contributions and from money generated by the sale of goods and services. The surplus of the member's labor (food and clothing, for example) either produced individually or in branch-sponsored businesses, would be placed in the depository in return for certificates of deposit, or "labor checks," equal to its value. Such paper could travel among members and nonmembers alike and could either be used for services or presented at the warehouse for those goods the holder desired. Each check would be backed by an item (stipulated on the front) that would at least equal the cash value of the face amount. As long as these notes circulated, their backing could not be removed from the depository without an equivalent being replaced or the artifacts themselves being returned for redemption. Unless they possessed these negotiable checks, nonmembers would pay cash for any depository acquisitions. And this income would be used exclusively for transactions with the "outside world." Theoretically, a person's earnings would be limited only by his industry, skill, and ability to produce.[10]

While the concept of the labor exchange foreshadows the modern notion of eliminating gold and silver as the basis for a circulating medium, the scheme De Bernardi put forward resembles that used by a conservative bank. Rather than requiring full specie backing of notes, the labor exchange substitutes goods. Consistent with this cautious philosophy, the national constitution refused to tolerate any potentially risky financial transactions. "The Association shall not borrow any money, and shall not issue any interest bearing note or obligation against itself." As De Bernardi himself proudly boasted, "financial failure is impossible." The overall inflationary impact of the labor-exchange plan was therefore limited since checks must equal the value of already existing depository items and there were no borrowed funds in its possession. The money supply, however, could have been expanded if certificates were issued in amounts exceeding their value or as obligations against anticipated depository acquisitions.[11]

How G. B. De Bernardi devised the concept of the labor exchange is unknown. The basic idea unquestionably existed before the publication of *Trials and Triumph of Labor*. The principal labor exchange organ, *Progressive Thought and Dawn of Equity,* for one, noted that "some of the Exchange plans were made use in England in 1833 to the great advantage of the laboring class." A subsequent issue contained a letter from Nebraskan James Iler who recalled that as head of his state's Grange executive committee in 1870, he had proposed a "like scheme to his associates, but [it] was too far in advance of the times for its adoption." While the English and Nebraska events might have been familiar to De Bernardi, his extensive reading may also have introduced him to the well-known activities of anarchist Josiah Warren. This former member of Robert Owen's utopian New Harmony, Indiana, launched a labor experiment in 1827 in Cincinnati, Ohio, that he called the "Equity Store." Warren's short-lived cooperative concern employed a variation of the labor check in a system where the exchange of goods and services was based solely on cost. More likely the labor exchange founder encountered either the literature or the supporters (many of whom came from Kansas City) of Albert Kimsey Owen's famed Mexican cooperative utopia of the 1880s, the Credit Foncier Company, located at Topolobampo harbor (Pacific City) in Siñaloa. Owen rejected the traditional medium of exchange based on precious metals; like Josiah Warren, he adopted an alternative one established on goods and services. Owen's company, however, called its paper notes "units of accounts" rather than "labor checks."[12]

*Looking Backward,* Edward Bellamy's famous 1888 blueprint of the perfect society, conceivably influenced De Bernardi on money matters. As one of the most popular works of the times, often selling over a thousand copies daily, this utopian novel had an enormous impact upon the era's reformers. While Bostonians of 2000 A.D. used neither "units of accounts" nor "labor checks," they functioned in a moneyless economy. These fortunate souls had solved the problem of an inadequate and inequitable circulating medium. Every individual received the same yearly income transferable through a credit-card system. Explained the book's Dr. Leete:

> A credit corresponding to his share of the annual product of the nation is given to every citizen on the public books at the beginning of each year, and a credit card issued him with which he procures at the public storehouses, found in every community, whatever he desires whenever he desires it. This arrangement, you will see, totally obviates the necessity for

business transactions of any sort between individuals and consumers.

Theoretically, if the Bellamy scheme worked in futuristic America, it could operate successfully during the closing years of the nineteenth century.[13]

Irrespective of the merits, limitations, or exact origins of the labor exchange, this brainchild of G. B. De Bernardi initially found few supporters. But as the depression deepened, the poor, especially factory workers and miners, started to consider the De Bernardi blueprint. His band of lecturers attracted large and enthusiastic crowds. Agrarians generally did not join. While they might support local cooperatives and political reform, the labor exchange usually was not practical. Explained one Plains farmer, "We can't make the L. E. beneficial to us. We are a little inland town [Leola, South Dakota] where there is nothing manufactured and but little raised except wheat."[14]

The De Bernardi proposal naturally interested those troubled individuals who viewed it as a temporary haven from the vicissitudes of the day. Others, unmistakably in a minority, shared the founder's notions that the labor exchange needed to become a permanent feature on the American scene. As an alternative, even a possible substitute to capitalism, it could be "the best plan for the dawning of the new industrial era; . . . a system that will guarantee protection in times of trouble and permit each working person every day to gain a fair and living wage in up-to-date shops and factories." There were other advantages. "If our system is carried out," reasoned one exchange propagandist, "it will save thousands [of] dollars of the criminal and pauper taxes." And another attraction: the labor exchange "will encourage the able to work . . . for they will always know that jobs will be there and they will not have to fret about their fate." Similarly, the plan would be a vast improvement over those contemporary conditions that caused heartache and pain due to economic inequalities. A California supporter expressed this idea nicely: "The Labor Exchange will be the foundation for true religion—the religion of humanity; because it changes our system so it will be possible for us to do right."[15]

While believing in self-help, supporters of the labor exchange did not eschew politics. As Plains and Southland agrarians flocked to the banners of the Farmers' Alliance and the subsequent People's party, workers, too, gave their blessings to the populist revolt

and parallel urban-based reform movements. The dominant sentiment among the rank and file, however, was a general skepticism
about the immediate value of the political approach. De Bernardi,
as seen earlier, held out little hope for triumphs at the polls. Perhaps the best expression of this pessimistic view of political possibilities came from the pen of Anna Walder, a South Dakota Exchanger and Populist. Writing in late 1897, she concluded: "The
only way to insure liberty and prosperity to all is to boycott the
money power by L. E. methods. To wait for Congress, with its
nothings and scoundrels, to make laws that would benefit the
masses and to wait for the initiative and referendum to operate is a
vain hope. . . ." Even though Walder represented the prevalent attitude among exchange members that the Jacob S. Coxey non-
interest-bearing road bonds "would have been just the thing," she
saw that the likelihood of getting national lawmakers to approve
such legislation "would be like the mice in the fable wanting to put
a bell on the cat in order to hear her when she comes." The labor
exchange, of course, could be placed into operation almost immediately. "We believe in political action," concluded the editor of
*Progressive Thought and Dawn of Equity,* "but the remedy lies not
there." And with the 1896 triumph of William McKinley and the
Republicans over William Jennings Bryan and his coalition of
"popocrats," the labor exchange gained more popularity as re-
form-oriented individuals asked themselves, "Who does not admit
that even relief is hopeless through political movement?"[16]

While the precise number of labor exchange participants is unrecorded, the crusade grew rapidly after the Panic of 1893. The
greatest surge came in 1896–1897 as the idea spread, the organizational groundwork was laid, and the uselessness of political action
became more widely believed. By depression's end De Bernardi's
scheme claimed more than 15,000 followers in approximately 325
branch organizations. Units appeared in all sections of the country,
but most were concentrated in the West and Midwest. While virtually autonomous, these locals received guidance from the central
office located in Independence, Missouri.[17]

THE EXPERIENCES of three labor exchange branches in Ohio superbly
illustrate not only the practicality but also the variations and refine-
ments of the De Bernardi concept. These "Buckeye state" exchangers, moreover, enjoyed considerable success. Like typical ones nationally, their histories can be measured in years and not months.

Ohio as a whole did not suffer as badly as some places during the depression. Its diversified and mature agricultural base maintained reasonable levels of rural income. The state's numerous dairymen, in particular, were affected less than other kinds of farmers elsewhere, and the price of their products fluctuated the least. Indeed, dairy receipts were the last to fall and the first to rise when recovery began.[18]

Even so, Ohioans felt the sting of economic dislocation. Especially hard hit were inhabitants of factory towns, transportation centers, and coal mining camps. Although unemployment figures are incomplete, the rate appears uniformly high. Akron is representative. Even though this bustling community of 27,000 enjoyed a mixed industrial base, highlighted by farm machinery, cereal, and clay-products manufacturing, unemployment soared by 1894 to over 3,400 out of an estimated work force of approximately 6,400. And this high rate continued until the eve of the Spanish-American War.[19]

The Cincinnati local emerged as Ohio's pioneer labor exchange unit. Dating from 1893, it preceded by several years the founding of sister exchanges in Ohio. From the beginning, the "Queen City" branch established a depository and embarked upon a program of manufacturing. Soon the local made such diverse products as buggies and brooms and even entered the house-remodeling business, paying crews with checks. These paper certificates had value. Reported one newspaper in early 1896, "their checks are good in seventy-five business houses in the city, so that the members can buy anything they need with their own checks."[20]

Hundreds of the more than seven thousand unemployed locally found a new lease on life. "Many hopeless men," observed Cincinnatian R. H. Thornbury, "were encouraged on their journey through life by being helped to help themselves in becoming members of the Exchange." And he added, "Many widdows [sic], in very poor circumstances were given work at fair rates." Concluded a local minister, "The L. E. has saved the city, something the politicians have not done." Indeed, an unresponsive political system might thus be successfully circumvented.[21]

The Cincinnati unit confronted hard times in ways other than the use of labor checks. The published thoughts of De Bernardi did not restrict branch members like a straitjacket; members developed pragmatic solutions to specific needs. In the city's east end, for example, Exchangers pitched a tent on a lot of a fellow member where "worthy idle men are aided to grub . . . during their enforced idleness." This soup kitchen relied on both an exchange-sponsored community garden and charitable donations to underwrite the average weekly cost of $1.25 per person. In a highly imaginative fashion the branch organized two squads of six men each to fish around the clock from the banks of the Ohio River. So the hungry had more than bread and water and seasonal vegetables.[22]

For intellectual nourishment, the Cincinnati exchange attached a free reading room to its depository building at the corner of Sixth and Lock Streets. The library boasted a "complete stock of L. E. and reform literature and other good books." Exchange proponents firmly believed that self-help meant more than providing the necessities of life; the spread of the labor exchange gospel was to be a fundamental task. Just as proponents of the larger Progressive movement saw education as an essential ingredient for uplift, so did these Cincinnatians. "We must be the practical alternative to the exploitation of trusts and we can change America *only* if people are informed."[23]

The twilight period of the Cincinnati Labor Exchange is hazy. The organization disappeared by the end of the nineties. The membership presumably melted away into the larger society as prosperity once again returned to the "Queen City." The desire for reform conceivably found expression through other outlets, likely in the city's developing socialist crusade.[24]

The labor exchange idea helped the unemployed of Toledo, as it did the brethren in Cincinnati. Launched in 1895, Local Sixty-five viewed itself as "the fastest and surest conduit through which the community might assist the working class poor." Toledo exchange President-Treasurer W. C. Hopkins outlined the needs in a public broadside: "Many persons are in destitute circumstances and their families suffering by no fault of theirs. They want work, but cannot procure it. If you doubt this, come and look at our books." While precise data are unavailable, the Hopkins reference to "many" being unemployed accurately depicts conditions in this lakefront community of 80,000. Writing to the United States Commissioner of Labor in June 1897, Mayor Samuel M. Jones observed, "The industrial depression is so great in this city and surrounding country that I am lead [*sic*] to conclude that the number of men in enforced idleness at the present time is greater perhaps . . . than at any other time in our history."[25]

Although the Toledo Labor Exchange opened a depository

and headquarters at Adams and Water Streets, it did little manufacturing. Apparently Local Sixty-five never made buggies, baskets, brooms, or bedsteads. Extant treasurers' reports reveal that
supporters individually brought various items, mainly food and
clothing, to the warehouse for checks. The several hundred members and other participants relied much more fully on trading work;
for instance, washing and ironing clothes for carpentry chores;
plumbing for music lessons; odd jobs for shelter.[26]

Since the Toledo exchange bartered services rather than goods,
the return of better times helped to promote its swift demise. The
structure of Local Sixty-five was easy to dismantle; members could
more conveniently walk away from service agreements than on-
going businesses.

The Toledo Labor Exchange never really sought to institutionalize the De Bernardi concept. The "conduit" philosophy and service orientation are principal reflections of this attitude. Permanent
change seemed imminent through political action. The compassionate and charismatic mayor, "Golden Rule" Jones, did much to
coopt the Exchangers. In reality, the mayor and not the labor exchange could best serve Toledo. From 1897 until his death in July
1904, Jones and his administration actively sought not only to help
depression victims but to bring about fundamental changes in the
community's political and economic life. "I believe that any man
who is willing to work has a right to life," argued the mayor, "and
I am doing my best to make such conditions as will grant to every
man who is willing to work the privilege to do so."[27]

Based on existing evidence, the Toledo local harbored no ill
will, only fondness and admiration toward the Jones administration. "I see our objectives being met [with the mayor]," wrote
President Hopkins in late 1898, "and I see political action as the
salvation for those down on their luck, but the idea of the L. E. is
good although not the only one for general improvement." Another member elaborated. He concluded that the principal mission
for this exchange was to be ready again if conditions should warrant its work. "It's an insurance policy," a cogent summary of one
of the labor exchange's inherent values. "We may require the Exchange at sometime in the future, I don't know for one never
knows when boodlers and special interests will recapture the city
and economic calamity will confront us." The Toledo Exchange
soon faltered. Rather than becoming semidormant and ready for
expansion, Number Sixty-five disappeared entirely by the turn of
the century.[28]

One hundred and thirty miles to the east, Akronites made traditional adjustments to hard times. They slashed public and private spending, planted community gardens, and relied upon the good works of charities. Some enthusiastically embraced the tenets of the labor exchange. Assisted by P. F. O'Neil of Branch 84, a flourishing local in Ashtabula, a core of out-of-work Akron factory men received a charter in late 1896 for Branch 191. The unit opened in January 1897 with 58 members, and it grew rapidly, claiming 156 backers by June, and 187 two months later.[29]

Prospects seemed promising. The local press applauded the De Bernardi experiment in its midst. As the dominant Republican organ editorialized, "No opportunity was better offered to the worthy needy of Akron whereby they might help themselves, depending on their own skill rather than charity." Akron merchants, hard pressed by the bad times, accepted the labor exchange. Unlike tradesmen in some localities, they frequently took labor checks. And these businessmen universally welcomed employment of the idle. While some would face commercial competition from a thriving labor exchange local, they believed that this was far superior to the potential damage from a hungry, angry mob.[30]

A beehive of activity characterized the initial year of Branch 191. From its 24 × 50-foot depository near the corner of Center and Main Streets near the downtown hub, the local launched broom-making and cobbler departments. The manufacturing of baskets and crates, hats and leather goods soon followed. Branch officials also announced plans for a grist mill and brickyard, and they happily noted that "more Akron merchants will accept LE checks." The headquarters structure itself became a "veritable trading post or department store." To assist further the community's unemployed, the organization kept a careful listing of those individuals who desired work and claimed that it could supply any type of labor, skilled or unskilled.[31]

While the Akron local enjoyed an initial period of success, difficulties came to haunt it. As with sister labor exchange branches in Ohio and elsewhere, rapidly improving economic conditions siphoned off supporters. But a principal reason for the demise of Branch 191 was its undertaking of a highly controversial railroad-building project.

In July 1897, exchange leaders started negotiations with H. B. Camp, a nearby Wooster businessman, to build a fourteen-mile rail line in the New Philadelphia area, about fifty miles south of Akron. This artery would presumably provide local shippers with a much needed outlet for their agricultural products and give them greater leverage with the region's entrenched steam carriers, who supported the powerful rate pool known officially as the Central States Traffic Association. According to the Camp-Labor Exchange agreement, Akron members would also assist in the construction of several grain elevators along the proposed route.[32]

Presumably, the Exchangers would receive checks for their labors. Promoter Camp, however, would not create a depository to redeem these obligations, but rather he would deposit securities with the Akron branch. The local could then dispose of these negotiable instruments as it saw fit; ideally it would acquire more warehouse items for redemption purposes or for expansion of its manufacturing activities.

The rail scheme did not remain a paper or hot-air one. During the fall of 1897 actual roadbed grading began, with more than a dozen Akron men at work with picks and shovels, teams, and scrapers. But before the roadbed was completed and the steel and crossties laid, internal dissent erupted among the membership. A sizable number thought the railroad undertaking was too grandiose and risky, suggesting instead expansion of the already successful broom-making business and entry into bedspring manufacturing.[33]

While little is known of events during the declining years of Branch 191, dissension caused by the rail project and debate over its overall objectives, coupled with more prosperous conditions and later to the absence of a skilled business manager, crippled the Akron experiment. Still, a limited membership continued to function into the early years of the twentieth century. The last recorded reference occurs in 1906.[34]


THE LABOR EXCHANGE CONCEPT offered a possible and palatable cure for society's ills. Yet the experiences of the three Ohio branches testify to the seemingly transitory character of the De Bernardi scheme. The unemployed may have been attracted to this "common sense response to hard times," but a return of prosperity showed their interest to be as fleeting as a summer rainbow. Indeed, De Bernardi designed the labor exchange to be a loose-knit, self-help institution that fostered individualism. "[A member] can work where he pleases and how he pleases, and his interest in whatever he may do for the Labor Exchange will always be kept to his credit, and no third party can buy, beg, borrow or steal that interest."[35]

How does a self-help device become permanent? This fundamental question confronted those who saw the labor exchange as the way to reorient American capitalism and provide protection from future downswings. After all, the labor exchange plan lacked government sponsorship, and the unemployed, more concerned with their immediate plight, regularly abandoned the cause when prosperity returned.

G. B. De Bernardi recognized the problem. His major writings suggest that once labor exchange depositories and their satellite enterprises became on-going concerns, membership would flourish. Steady growth and the interchange of goods and services between locals over the years, he believed, would ensure the movement's permanence. De Bernardi took great stock in the "nothing succeeds like success" adage. While neither he nor prominent figures within the exchange specifically described the scheme's ultimate form, the anticipated outcome would be either a system parallel to existing capitalism or ideally its eventual replacement. Perhaps the federal government would step in, establish depositories, and make checks on stored products legal tender for all public and private transactions. "We should expect to ultimately have the one big people ['s] trust like Mr. Bellamy described where L. E. industries and checks represent all business and all money," speculated one Exchanger. "The arrogant trusts and the money powers would be through." In the same vein, another member thought this self-help crusade was "a step in the right direction—that is towards State Socialism." If Farmers' Alliance and Populist party folks could hope for Washington officials to grant them their beloved sub-treasury system and eventually realize that aim, labor exchangers then could have a similar objective—a program within rather than outside government.[36]

This question of how to institutionalize the labor exchange emerged as the principal schism within the movement. A minority firmly felt that the creation of individual worker colonies held the key. De Bernardi blasted such a suggestion; he fervently opposed formation of isolated rural labor settlements. This issue became so important that he wrote a slim volume, *Colonizing in a Great City,* to make known his position. When published in 1897, it coincided with the much-publicized and potentially successful efforts of Eugene V. Debs to launch a cooperative commonwealth colony in Washington state for the unemployed. De Bernardi utilized his book to condemn those who favored separate communities rather than integrated urban exchanges. "The Colony idea won't work," he scoffed, "because the ones who need it worst, will never on earth be able to reach the all-evasive dollars and even if they were, there are all of the hardships of pioneer life to endure." On the other hand, De Bernardi contended, the urban setting continued to offer labor uplifters splendid opportunities to improve society.[37]

Notwithstanding the official position on colony building, opponents within the movement argued that by depression's end "the only real hope of making the Labor Exchange *permanent,* something more than just a passing response to hard times, is through colonies. . . ." Settlements could continue to demonstrate the advantages of the labor exchange alternative, and as living testimonials to De Bernardi's insights, this self-help concept would be there for emulation if economic disaster again struck. This reasoning parallels the thought of contemporary proponents of city-owned land who saw such property as being instant garden space if depression recurred. Two labor exchange colonies appeared, closely linked.[38]

The September 1896 issue of *Progressive Thought* described formation of the first labor exchange settlement. In the isolated Arkansas Ozarks seven miles from Berryville, seat of Carroll County, and twenty-eight miles from Eureka Springs, the nearest railroad station, several families imbued with exchange principles soon controlled two-hundred acres. Although the colony's formation annoyed the national leadership, the separatists became Local Eighty-two. Perhaps they received their charter because their leader, Frank W. Cotton, had loyally served the movement as an organizer and because they were so few in number. Admittedly, once in operation chartered branches enjoyed carte blanche rights anyway.[39]

"Maple," as the Arkansas colony was commonly called, failed to grow much during its one-year life. Its assets were scanty: "Four-room log house . . . , frame house in course of erection; several outbuildings; orchard of 1000 trees; [and] 30 acres of land cleared and fenced." The main colony industries, fruit raising and stone quarrying, supposedly could supply the necessary sources of income, labor checks and cash. But certain drawbacks such as "distance from RR, rough roads, pebbly character of soil" convinced Cotton and his tiny band to seek a more favorable site.[40]

On March 8, 1897, a handful of colony enthusiasts, including the former Arkansans who had dissolved Local 82, gathered in the farmhouse of James and John Howard in Freedom township, Bourbon County, Kansas, to launch the second labor exchange community. Officially chartered as Local 199, this settlement of former railroaders, coal miners, and farmers became known as "Freedom." Like Maple, "Freedom is disliked by De Bernardi and others," wrote one member, "but [they] can't prevent us from operating under the Exchange principal [*sic*]." (And there is no indication that they did.) He added the supposition that "I suggest that they are pleased that we are not abandoning the message of the *Trials and Triumph of Labor*."[41]

Freedom's founders agreed to locate the colony on land owned by the Howards. The brothers were to sell sixty acres for a townsite at low cost; additional land would be leased at reasonable rates. Cheap real estate therefore saved the Freedomites' money (always in limited supply) that they could use to implement their plans. Fortunately, the Howard farm contained "coal, oil, natural gas and other natural deposits of value," and its location in the heart of the state's mineral belt (and near other exchanges) enhanced the site's value.[42]

With a nucleus of a dozen members, the Freedom Labor Exchange surveyed a townsite and divided adjoining land into farm plots. Colonists quickly constructed tar-paper shanties and dugouts, started several cottage industries, and planted field crops. Life was rugged for the settlers during the first months, especially during the winter; the next year, 1898, John Howard painted this hopeful picture of colony life:

> We have raised a very good crop. [John W.] Fitzgerald and us boys put in 15 acres of cane and it looks nice—some is ready to make up. . . . We started a shaft to the coal the 4th of July and reached the coal day before yesterday. Have a good quality of coal in a vein 24 inches thick. So we have coal and hedge posts to redeem check[s] with, and if nothing happens, we will have sorghum next week.[43]

These hardy colonists seemingly shared a common world view. Foremost, as indicated, they saw Freedom as the sensible means of perpetuating the labor exchange concept, "the glue to keep us together." But also there is evidence suggesting that the settlement might serve as the nucleus for political action. The time seemed ripe. Freedom emerged when the Populist organization was rapidly crumbling and before the Socialist movement enjoyed its impressive growth. "We can fill the [reform] void," argued John Fitzgerald in 1899, "and use the ballot box to take the country [county appeared to be a better possibility!] in the interests of the unemployed and ruined souls." (The Freedomites were thus planning a strategy identical to that sought during the depression of the 1930s by the Reverend Mr. A. J. Muste and his worker-followers— the so-called Musterites—to turn individuals, down on their luck and dependent on self-help, into a militant political force.) Few in numbers, the political ambitions of Local 199 came to little. Several members ran for county offices, albeit unsuccessfully, and the precinct backed liberal candidates; Populists and later Socialists collected numerous votes in contests held between 1898 and 1904.[44]

While failing to achieve its objectives, Freedom reached its zenith during the early months of the twentieth century. Population peaked at more than thirty and the experiment achieved considerable notoriety. This tiny Kansas settlement, however, came to public attention not for its economic blueprint, but rather for its flying-machine factory. Not only did this ill-conceived project flop totally, but recurring financial problems, internal personality disputes, and newspaper charges of "free-love" practices led to the colony's disintegration by 1905.[45]


EVEN THOUGH a discernible split about the practicality of colony experiments developed within labor exchange ranks, on the whole the movement encountered little outside opposition. Actually, a fundamental flaw in the labor exchange crusade was too little publicity. Concluded one labor journalist in 1897, "At a time when the discussion of economic questions was never so active this factor of labor exchanges has asserted itself so quietly that their very existence is unknown to probably nine-tenths of the people of the United States." Opposition was unlikely for yet another reason. Exchangers repeatedly emphasized their abiding faith in the work ethic and in America itself. They could not accept "willful idlers," and they disagreed with one Populist who concluded in 1895 that "A period of anarchy and revolution is inevitable. I have spent my time and money freely in the reform movement . . . but now give it up as lost."[46]

A consistent response to the labor exchange's existence quickly emerged. The average person who knew but disapproved of the De Bernardi concept typically ignored it. Instances exist in which merchants objected to competition spawned by exchange industries, but acts of outright hostility are unrecorded. Reform types generally gave lip service to the merits of the labor exchange; few openly opposed it. Admittedly, some contemporary uplifters thought the notion impractical or misguided. A Cleveland, Ohio, Socialist and cooperative store enthusiast, for instance, suggested that the labor exchange's desire to "produce something" illustrated the "cart before the horse" principle, arguing that this method accumulated goods for which no market existed. Instead, he noted that his pet self-help organization, the Cleveland Industrial Co-operative Society, "works on surer and more business like basis: we are sure of a market before we buy our goods, the wisdom of which policy cannot be questioned."[47]

The colony approach to institutionalizing the labor exchange failed miserably. But the De Bernardi method itself did not prove to be a stunning success. Although this self-help scheme was transitory, still it cannot be dismissed as a failure. For one thing, the vast majority of local branches lasted through the depression years. The exchange's supportive services during a time of extreme economic dislocations gave thousands of down-on-their-luck Americans opportunities to acquire both the necessities of life and self-respect. By its very existence the labor exchange promised a more humane economic system and gave hope for a better society. Observed a Cheyenne, Wyoming, resident, "I have been working in the reform movement for years, but it strikes me that by these labor exchanges we have got the Monopoly Bull by the horns and he can't help himself." Furthermore, the presence of these branches at a crucial point in the nation's history conceivably lessened class violence. Likely they served as a type of safety valve. "While we never attracted that many to our cause, we satisfied many troubled men and women," wrote an ex-Exchanger. "Word of our successes surely gave hope and solace to so many more." And there may be truth in his conclusion that "we did much to save this country from a bloody revolt." Having a definite plan for action probably helped defuse the anger and anguish of the unemployed by focusing their efforts on seemingly achievable results.[48]

The labor exchange episode is more than merely an illustration of self-help in the classic mold. It aptly reveals how bands of poor people, determined to assist themselves, might respond. What the advocates of the De Bernardi plan did was to encourage the jobless to shoulder the burden of depression themselves by launching their own support network *outside* the economic system. The logical alternative—the goal, for example, of the Coxeyites and later the Musterites and one even endorsed by some Exchangers—stressed the responsibility of government to provide a remedy to hard times.

The demand centered on forcing the economic structure to produce useful, full-time work at a decent wage. Whether the labor exchange approach is an example of an outmoded individualism is debatable. But as shown earlier, the De Bernardi strategy may well have been the more practical of the two responses to "Work, Not Dole!" Not only did Coxey fail completely, but the down-and-out generally were unsuccessful in pressing for meaningful changes in the economic policies of government, particularly at the federal level.[49]

# Cooperative Stores

H A T is co-operation if it is not self help?"
asked the *Omaha World-Herald* in 1894. Indeed
it was. Other than community gardens, the ever-
popular cooperative business became the single
most widely attempted self-help response to hard
times. Unlike either the Pingree Potato Patch or
the labor exchange, mutual group buying or selling of a product or service had long been a familiar
practice. During the early 1870s, for example, the National Grange of the Patrons of Husbandry, America's leading
farm order of the day, did more than lash out at railroad abuse;
members enthusiastically embraced cooperative thought through
an assortment of enterprises. These ranged from hardware and implement outlets, to creameries, and life-and fire-insurance companies. The latter proved especially successful. Wisconsin farmers, in
particular, took to heart the official state Grange request: "Patrons, you cannot afford to pay these high premiums to joint stock
companies. Insure yourselves and keep some money at home." By
the 1880s Wisconsin emerged as the banner place for this form of
dependable, low-cost protection.[1]

When the economic crunch of the late 1880s severely squeezed
Dixie and Plains plowmen, expansion of existing farmer marketing
and retailing cooperatives occurred. In a more revealing way, hundreds of new ones appeared. The economic creed of the National
Farmers' Alliance and Industrial Union, that vanguard of political
populism which spread rapidly across the Southland in the mid-
eighties and soon spilled onto the parched prairies, contained a fer-
vent commitment to cooperativism, both as a means for immediate
self-help and ultimately as a plausible alternative to the incumbent
form of capitalism. The structural organization of the Alliance,
with cohesive local units that provided meaning and direction to
members experiencing the trauma of the times, allowed for the

growth of mutual concepts. As Robert C. McMath, Jr. so aptly shows in his examination of the movement:

> The network of subordinate, county, and state Alliances, along with the subsidized press, offered an ideal setting for instruction in the techniques of cooperation. . . . the fraternity intensity of the sub-alliance meetings and the evangelical fervor of Alliance rallies provided a social setting in which farmers could be persuaded to commit themselves to unproved economic programs.[2]

Even with the dual strengths of need and organization, most Alliance cooperatives proved short-lived, failing by the early 1890s. While these concerns often produced savings on such high-demand items as fertilizer and cotton bagging, inadequate capitalization, inefficient management, credit problems, and continuation of the farm depression brought collapse. Although the vast majority of Alliance stores had closed their doors permanently by the time of the Panic of 1893, ex-members frequently endorsed the rhetoric of mutualism for years to come.[3]

Yet the general failure of the cooperative business segment of the Farmers' Alliance did not mean that all mutual agricultural enterprises died by the nineties. In fact, new ones emerged. The most famous were two marketing organizations, the Chautauqua and North East Grape Association of New York formed in early 1892 (reorganized as the Chautauqua and Erie Grape Company five years later), and the citrus Sunkist Growers of California launched in 1895. Significantly, many farming communities were forced to maintain certain mutual operations due to the refusal of commercial firms to provide the service either because of risk or low volume, hence a poor rate of return on investment capital. Still, some cooperatives enjoyed remarkably good financial health. As one Illinois editor noted in 1895:

> The farmers in our country for many years have been making advances in various lines of cooperation. Hundreds upon hundreds of prosperous ones dot the countryside in the Middle West. . . . The application of the principle of co-operative insurance has met with the most marked success of late. It seems that about every farming district has its own heavily patronized mutual company.

He should have mentioned another popular cooperative activity, the spectacular triumph of farmer-owned cheeseries and creameries.[4]

Cooperative cheese- and butter-making firms had been common since the antebellum years. Without doubt they offered significant advantages over home production. Cheese and butter factories could process products and distribute them much more efficiently than could individual farmers. The typical agrarian needed a dependable outlet for surplus milk, but often his production volume was insufficient to warrant domestic cheese making. The manufacturing of cheese in particular was a time-consuming and a generally unpleasant task. And there was usually minimal competition from investor-owned operations. Since the average creamery was a low-volume affair due to the generally poor quality of transportation services, decentralized facilities dominated the industry. Yet these concerns operated on "the scale that best brings about handsome profits, for even during difficult times such products remain in strong demand." While families might make enormous sacrifices, milk for the children remained a priority purchase. Then, of course, the cooperative meant producer control. "Dairy co-operatives," concluded the *Ohio Farmer* in 1896, "bring producer say in policies."[5]

The Milbank Co-operative Creamery Association, located in northeastern South Dakota, illustrates the thousands of durable late nineteenth century farmer mutual enterprises. Launched by several scores of Grant County milk producers in the mid-1880s, "to help ourselves with a task that individually we could not perform," this concern sported the traditionally simple structure. The arrangement between the farmer and the cooperative management went as follows:

> In consideration of the patrons furnishing milk to be manufactured into butter, the managers agree to manufacture the butter and find the best market possible for said butter, and at the end of the month they will pay IN CASH to the patrons . . . every cent there is left from the sale of butter, after deducting the expense of manufacturing the butter and getting it to market.[6]

This community venture quickly established a brisk, profitable trade, due largely to an aggressive and unusually talented management. By the midnineties Milwaukee Railroad freight and express cars carried the association's dairy products into the region's immediate marketplaces. Regular customers appeared in Sioux Falls, Sioux City, Minneapolis, and St. Paul. Not surprising, the cooperative enjoyed strong farmer support. "The patrons of the creamery include Populists, Democrats, Republicans, Prohibitionists, greenbackers, silverites, and all shades of religious belief," reported the *Grant County Review* a decade after the cooperative's founding. "The farmers in this community are more vitally interested in this enterprise than in any other enterprise that has been established in this community." Goodwill existed for an easily fathomable reason: "Every cent of the profit over and above the actual operating expenses goes to the farmers who furnish the milk. . . ." And in a closely related fashion, the creamery "has had the tendency to increase the number of cows kept on the farms which calls for more grass land and thereby decreases the acreage of land devoted to producing virtually worthless corn and wheat." This particular cooperative continued to provide Milbank area dairymen benefits until its closing in the 1940s.[7]

THE TRYING TIMES of the 1890s depression prompted urban dwellers to follow the cooperative trails blazed by rural residents. "We had better pay attention to what the Alliance has done with their exchanges," concluded a Baltimore cigar maker in 1893. "Group buying for workers seems just the ticket for assisting ourselves to get ahead. . . ." He added, "I see co-operative stores as a practical way to an immediately better life for those in want." The Reverend Mr. R. Heber Newton of Chicago told fellow Methodists the same year, "I am surprised at the slight interest taken by the city people of this country in co-operative and industrial associations. These are reforms, at least, in which Europeans lead us a long way." He pointed out that such self-help arrangements enjoyed widespread popularity in the Old World. "There are 2,380 co-operative societies in Germany with a membership of over 1,000,000. . . . In England there are 1,180 societies, with 600,000 members. . . ." Reverend Newton noted that "these associations have buyers in every large market in the world, who are ever on the alert to take advantage of a decline in prices," and he correctly prophesied that "the benefits to be derived from these organizations are so obvious that the time cannot be far distant when they will become common here, as they undoubtedly should be."[8]

Perhaps the Reverend Mr. Newton was unaware of the efforts of America's premier labor organization of the 1880s, the Knights of Labor, at launching cooperative businesses during its period of rapid expansion. The Knights attempted a full range of cooperative experiments: producer cooperatives like a member-owned coal mine near Cannelburg, Indiana, that debuted in 1884 or the National Knights of Labor Co-operative Tobacco Company begun in Raleigh, North Carolina, two years later; and consumer ones like the T. V. Powderly Cooperative Association, a general store, started in March 1887 at a cooperative Knights of Labor community, Powderly, near Birmingham, Alabama; or the Dubuque, Iowa, Knights Co-operative Grocery that opened several months later. Actually, the national order did little to implement its mutual theories. Members, moveover, seemed interested only when the economy faltered after 1884; with the return of better times, support for these self-help enterprises flagged. Those widely scattered cooperatives that did emerge nearly all vanished by the early nineties, usually for the same reasons that brought demise to the Alliance mutual ventures. Even the sponsoring organization foundered by this time, for the Knights gave way to the "business unionism" of the American Federation of Labor.[9]

After the Panic of 1893 struck, the national press reported more extensively and frequently on the possibilities of cooperative activities. Coverage included stories of both foreign and domestic experiments. Although few journalists saw this economic arrangement as a potential challenge to the country's established business structure, virtually all recognized the immediate benefits of cooperative action. As often happens during a time of crisis, ideas that had either been largely ignored or thought foolish gained greater interest and respectability. Rochdale stores and Mormon Church enterprises were two such examples.

On a rainy night in November 1843 twelve hard-pressed tradesmen—weavers, hatters, and tailors—who lived in Rochdale, in the industrial Midlands of England, developed the concept of the modern cash cooperative store, their Rochdale Equitable Pioneer Society. Popularly called the "Rochdale Plan," the idea was to operate a business concern, usually a general store, wholly in the economic interests of the patrons. As often constructed, a Rochdale operation charged backers a small entrance fee and subsequently sold them stock, normally for 10 percent down, with the balance payable from anticipated dividends. Although a portion of the profits went into a reserve fund, the operation credited the remainder to members as dividends proportional to their purchases. Prices on goods were kept at the lowest possible levels. Thus a shareholder profited from patronizing the business as well as from owning stock. The Rochdale concern ideally would eventually expand the scope of its operation (launching industries, even selling real estate), therefore further adding to the supporter's pocketbook and also stimulating employment opportunities.[10]

Although the generally recognized flaw in the Rochdale scheme (and one emphasized repeatedly by the proponents of the labor exchange) centered on the inability of potential patrons to pay both an initiation charge and stock assessments, the *New York World,* for one, listed its merits. "We are in the midst of a national calamity," the paper reminded its readers in August 1894. "Anything and everything that can help the people of our nation to improve their economic lot are needed at once. . . . If a segment of society can afford to get a Rochdale store started, many can be assisted." Revealing the plan's earlier existence, the *World* noted, "The National Grange brought it [Rochdale] to our shores after the Civil War, and it aided their followers during a previous period of hard times. . . . It can do the same nowadays." This, too, was essentially the structure of the ill-fated Knights of Labor urban cooperatives.[11]

While the number of Rochdale stores launched during the aftermath of the panic is unrecorded—the total probably exceeds several hundred—keen interest also developed in another cooperative story, the mutual business affairs of the Church of Jesus Christ of Latter-Day Saints, better known as the Mormons. Ever since the Church's beginnings in the early 1830s, this dynamic and resourceful religious sect enthusiastically practiced cooperative living; in fact, members initially adopted a form of communistic communitarianism.[12]

Although by the 1890s the average citizen likely knew of the Church only because of its much discussed practice of polygamy, newspapermen after the panic publicized the sect for an entirely different reason: Mormon economic experiences offered marvelous guides for practical self-help. Observed a writer for the politically conservative *Chicago Daily Inter-Ocean:* "The Mormon people began in the desert about forty years ago as a poverty stricken band of starvelings. They at once adopted a system of co-operation. . . . To-day they have wealth of over 600 million of dollars." The *Inter-Ocean* urged its readers to think: "While citizens may not want to join [the Church], its practices deserve a close scrutiny."[13]

The depression-era press frequently discussed two successful instances of Mormon self-improvement. The Church custom of tithing drew considerable attention. For the Saints, the act held special religious meaning. "By this principal it shall be seen whose hearts are set on doing the will of God and keeping His commandments, thereby sanctifying the land of Zion unto God." Not surprising, tithing produced enormous economic benefits for the closely knit membership. Whether in cash or in kind the Mormon people, usually through the General Tithing Office in Salt Lake City, generated enough real wealth to sustain and to expand the flock. Unquestionably, tithing became the chief means of capitalizing the Saints' economy, a technique remarkably similar to the English Rochdale system.[14]

The Mormon church's extensive sugar operations also attracted popular interest. Begun in the 1850s, this venture in agribusiness reveals superbly the cooperative spirit at work: thousands of individual members subscribed to stock of the Church-sponsored Utah Sugar Company and most selected its processed beet sugar for their domestic use. By the eighties Saints enjoyed a rewarding business in the classic self-help sense. Not only were they self-sufficient in sugar production, but many found employment in the firm's widespread activities throughout the Great Basin. Reported the *Integral Co-operator,* the voice of midwestern cooperativism, "[It] has been a 'sweet' success."[15]

AN EXAMINATION of two of the depression's cooperatives stores offers insights into the overall nature and purpose of this bootstrap response. Representative of the large-city mutual outlet is the one owned and operated by the Cleveland Industrial Co-operative Society. Indeed, it typified the urban cooperative adventure.

Hard times made Cleveland, Ohio, a city in trouble. A high percentage of its 1893 estimated population of 275,000 was unemployed; probably the lack of work reached two of every five adult males by the depression's depth during the winter of 1893–1894. "There's no employment here," became the ever-common lament. While the "Forest City" in time sported community gardens and several locals of the labor exchange, it also had at least one thriving mutual store.[16]

The Cleveland Industrial Co-operative Society came into being during the frantic days of the first "workless winter." While no single individual can take credit for its inception, Max S. Hayes, editor of the *Cleveland Citizen,* the city's chief labor paper, did much to boost the enterprise; he served as the society's president. While Hayes wanted workers and farmers to unite under the common banner of a reform political party "to set the country on the straight course," he, like the typical uplifter, recognized the need to "help the unemployed in an immediate fashion."[17]

The organization of the Cleveland cooperative store resembles the time-tested Rochdale scheme. "We are to use those notions of the English [Rochdale] plan that fit our circumstances," wrote edittor Hayes in November 1893. After all, the self-help programs of the day reflected the highly pragmatic philosophy that an idea means what an idea does. Like the Rochdale format, the Cleveland venture charged a membership fee—in this case a one-time payment of thirteen dollars. Stock was issued, but, differing from the model, a person was asked to pay the full par value; no certificates could be acquired "on time." If the store functioned properly, paid-up stockholders received semiannual cash or in-kind rebates. Yet not all profits would be distributed. In addition to an ongoing emergency money reserve, the society planned to expend some funds for educational purposes. Finally, as with all Rochdale businesses, prices on merchandise were extremely competitive; the store charged only a small markup to members and nonmembers alike.[18]

Without fanfare the society opened for business in February 1894. The site of its public outlet was a rented building at 446 Woodland Avenue, in the heart of the city's eastside working-class neighborhood. Drawing support mainly from trade unionists, it soon had about one hundred Clevelanders who joined and followed the advice of "Come and Do Business with Yourself." Groceries (flour, sugar, butter, and oatmeal) and coal became the major staples offered, although lines of hardware and oddments were subsequently added. To keep operating expenses to a minimum, merchandise was available only on Tuesdays from 4 P.M. to 10 P.M. After the enterprises became firmly established, the society planned to extend its hours, but this never occurred.[19]

Hard times brought a lively trade. Obviously the destitute and those who lived far away could not participate, but a sizable portion of the nearby populace could deal with the society; all patrons, of course, "wanted to watch every penny." As one customer reported: "The store is the only place where I can buy. For my family . . . this means so much. This bee-hive of activity on Tuesdays is so comforting." And he held the larger hope that some others shared, "Soon perhaps all commercial intercourse will be conducted in a like fashion, bad times or not." For about a year sales exceeded four hundred dollars weekly, and some "enthusiasts contemplated the erection of a block [of cooperative businesses.]"[20]

Expansion into other Cleveland neighborhoods became another idea that the society's membership repeatedly discussed during the early days. A flourishing cooperative store movement needed numerous outlets. "We must be near the people," backer John McVey argued. "[Street]car fare is to [*sic*] steep . . . and families can't send their sons on buying errands across town." Just as convenience food stores—the "7-11" variety—dot today's urban landscapes, alert cooperativists nearly ninety years ago recognized the value of what eventually proved to be a successful marketing device.[21]

Notwithstanding the potential of a sound merchandising strategy, the Cleveland store experienced a general decline as prosperity gradually returned. For many, its raison d'être vanished. "This place reminds me of a umbrella," remarked Valley Railroad and Terminal conductor J. W. Burkbeck, a three-year member, "its for a rainy day. Now [1898] that its gotten sunny I see no compelling reason to have it unless many jobs are lost." Perhaps conductor Burkbeck's unwillingness to continue support of the coming "Cooperative Age" stemmed from the severely limited business hours and range of items. As the store diminished in popularity, the inventory still featured food and fuel, but it was no shopper's paradise.[22]

Unlike the Burkbecks of the community, leader Max Hayes remained faithful. "[It] is a way to beat down the greedy capitalists for all times." But eventually even die-hards like Hayes conceded defeat. "In our highly developed capitalist system private cooperation, with limited means, cannot survive."[23]

The society liquidated its stock during the summer of 1898. When the final tally was made, members lost a portion of their investments. Only about 70 percent of the money paid into the operation was returned; stockholders got merchandise, not cash. Yet the sponsoring organization continued to function and in conjunction with the Central Labor Council for the next several years operated as an "Educational Society" dedicated to the spread of the "gospel of co-operation."[24]

This clinging to the mutual ideal by some Cleveland Industrial Co-operative Society supporters suggests that they viewed their self-help response as something more than a passing answer to hard times. While this dedicated core of "true believers" politically backed the new century's rapidly expanding Socialist party, they felt, in the words of Max Hayes:

> Depression has given us a chance to study carefully the workings of society and to see that they are sorely wanting. A brighter day for all will not dawn until people take over from the cold-hearted capitalists. Co-operative group efforts in commerce and at the ballot box will turn this land over to the people who are worthy of it.[25]

The desire to extend the advantages of cooperative buying to both an urban and rural constituency found expression in the St. Paul, Minnesota–based People's Hard Times Supply Company. This intriguing firm magnificently represents the self-help concept commonly known as syndicate buying. (Indeed, the notion was the other side of that self-help cooperative coin developed by the Farmers' Alliance in the 1880s—"cotton bulking"—in which producers pooled their crops and let an agent contact the large-scale buyers who then bid on the bales.) The syndicate idea had been used on an increasing basis by agrarians since the late eighties. In an 1893 paper, "Co-operation Among Farmers," N. O. Nelson, the well-known plumbing-supply manufacturer and tireless advocate of corporate profit sharing, outlined the scheme:

> [Commission] agents for some time have been in many parts of the country who arrange for wholesale prices on wagons, buggies, implements, organs, sewing machines, bicycles, and other goods of bulk value. A deposit is kept in the agent's hands to guarantee payment, and the goods are shipped C.O.D. direct to the consumer.[26]

In the fall of 1895, J. C. Hanley, a Twin Cities labor leader, sought to apply the syndicate-buying notion to the advantage of fellow workers and to offer it to area farmers as well. Through the backing of local trade unions and with the blessings of the nearly moribund Minnesota State Alliance, the People's Hard Times Supply Company was born. The cooperative heritage of St. Paul, combined with the tough times that "affects us all," may well have sparked the new scheme. Hanley, himself, said pointedly, "We can learn from those Swedes." He undoubtedly was alluding to a rather durable mutual business launched during the aftermath of the Panic of 1873 by the community's workingmen, most of whom had recently arrived from Scandinavia. Known fittingly as the "Swedish Cooperative Association," this bootstrap operation attracted considerable support, yet it closed in the early eighties. Probably interest waned and capital disappeared. As for the latter, representatives of the country's leading credit-rating firm, R. G. Dun, throughout the association's nearly decade of service, regularly reported money woes and issued such warnings as "credit should be given very sparingly" and "need[s] to be watched closely."[27]

Notwithstanding the ill-fated Swedish cooperative, the People's Hard Times Supply Company seemed determined to live; it had a mission to fulfill. As the masthead of its stationery proclaimed, "DIRECT FROM PRODUCER TO CONSUMER, WITHOUT WHOLESALERS' AND RETAILERS' PROFITS," the venture sought to "tackle the hard times with a sensible plan to make the dollar stretch as far as it is possible." Predictably for the leadership in the self-help crusade, Hanley expressed little hope with the political system. "Any speedy salvation for the people of the upper Miss[issippi] river valley will not likely come about at the ballot box. Even if there is a people's victory next year [1896] . . . that is a long time away." And understandably, he also viewed his association with the company as permanent. "Group buying is a workable device and its rewards can be enjoyed during boom times as well." It is not totally clear, however, what specific structure Hanley envisioned. Likely he was thinking in terms of the distribution practices then being widely discussed on the pages of the day's utopian literature. Futurist Henry Olerich, for one, called syndicate buying the "opening of the conduit of goods from the makers to the users without . . . fuss and expense."[28]

The actual structure of the People's Hard Times Supply Company displayed a highly streamlined flavor. This is revealed nicely when the start-up capital requirements are considered; only a few hundred dollars were required. From a makeshift office on East Eighth Street in St. Paul, the firm received orders from neighborhood agents who contracted patrons. "We have unemployed people, several of whom are out of work drummers, who have the knowledge and the disposition to seek out business." For their troubles, these representatives earned a modest commission of 2 percent on the amount of business generated. As with the growing mail-order industry, the supply company issued an extensive catalog. This volume allowed potential customers to choose merchandise from a dozen departments that ran the gamut from buggies to home-building materials. Paralleling other syndicate buying operations, the supply company sent the consigned goods directly to the consumer via COD express or freight. The agent's payment came directly from the small deposit required on every transaction.[29]

While records are incomplete, the People's Hard Times Supply Company appears to have done a relatively active business, at least during its formative period. In February 1896 volume totaled nearly $1,900, and the next month saw sales exceed $3,000. "March is an especially good trading time, for purchases for the Spring and Summer are customarily made at this time." With its staff of three volunteer office workers and nearly a dozen agents, the amount of trade in early 1896 probably taxed the organization to its limit. "We're busy as bees."[30]

In the tradition of kindred enterprises this self-help undertaking had special features. It developed an expansionist mood by entering directly into the cooperative store business. At a Twin Cities coalyard the supply company offered fuel at reduced rates to the general public. Although this particular service disappeared after two years, the St. Paul operation continued to seek to broaden its horizons; it joined with what proved to be a successful and durable cooperative grain elevator firm, the Farmers' Elevator Company. Started by southeastern Minnesota plowmen in the Goodhue County community of Zumbrota in 1894—"ones infected with Alliance thinking,"—the elevator initially served as a typical "line" grain buyer. But with an affiliation with the People's Hard Times Supply Company in late 1895, the Zumbrota enterprise acted as a direct outlet for a variety of bulk merchandise: coal, lumber, farm machinery, and later hardware, groceries, and drygoods.[31]

The commercial arrangements of what became the Farmers' Mercantile and Elevator Company retained much of the simplicity of the parent organizations. The St. Paul office made orders directly to manufacturers; goods were sent by rail to Zumbrota; and patrons, mostly farmers, then acquired them. But unlike a typical Rochdale store, customers could use their crops in lieu of cash; thus a type of barter emerged.[32]

The legal format proved to be a different matter. Originally, the organization of the Farmers' Elevator Company was not especially complicated. The capitalization totaled a modest $15,000, with seventy-eight charter investors holding an average of $200 worth of stock. The funds raised seemed adequate, for the enterprise kept construction costs low by utilizing considerable volunteer labor. When the bulk buyers entered the picture to add the mercantile dimension, they incorporated as a business under Minnesota law and acquired partial interest in the elevator. Heretofore, the

People's Hard Times Supply used "company" unofficially: it merely operated as an *ad hoc* concern.[33]

When syndicate buying ceased in 1898, the multifaceted activities of the elevator continued uninterrupted until the early 1920s, when it was crippled by the post–World War agricultural depression. Actually, the upswing in commodity prices by the late nineties, together with the company's overall efficiency and convenience, made operations profitable. "We are in good shape," announced the Farmers' Elevator in 1899. "Our practical program is working well. We do not require the services of bulking agents, and for that matter, city people no longer have to trouble themselves with this form of buying since the mills and factories are once again open."[34]

Still, the belief persisted that the entire business world should adopt the format of cooperative buying and selling. The report of the Zumbrota enterprise for 1901 included these thoughtful observations:

> Having been for seven years an earnest believer in co-operation, as the only certain and thorough remedy for the fate which stares us all in the face—that of being shut out from any other means of earning a livelihood than acting in the capacity of vassals of some immense aggregation of capital—it would seem that even the most loyal devotee of the Competitive System should begin to see that the best they are confronted with is the choice of but two alternatives in the future—either serving as the tool of monopoly or forming member-owned businesses like our Elevator. . . .[35]

Understandably, not everyone in southeastern Minnesota, or the entire nation for that matter, agreed with the philosophy of cooperativism. Local merchants howled at the competition from the Farmers' Mercantile and Elevator Company. In 1896, for example, area elevators conducted wholesale warfare against the mutualists. In one case they paid from two to three cents per bushel more for barley. The Farmers' Elevator, however, happily allowed this to occur; it "welcomes competition, especially when it is in the best interests of the farmer." Soon the rate cutting ended, but "some hard feelings continue."[36]

THE QUEST for cooperative business practices once more demonstrates the two-fold thrust of depression era self-help efforts. Throughout the country thoughtful respondents to harsh times gave a vitality to the long-standing idea of cooperative enterprises. Said a Colville, Washington, mutualist: "It is hard to get a dollar here; but these are the times that make me think, especially about the decades old co-operative approach which is the sensible approach." The Ohio and Minnesota case studies attest to the practicality of the concept as a suitable device to alleviate the economic stings of the day. As previously seen, the notion that this particular bootstrap scheme might be more than a temporary measure gained some currency. Although the "do-it-now" aspects enjoyed considerable popularity, proponents of a long-term change that would bring about a significantly better tomorrow drew loyal supporters too. But when prosperity returned, these souls found themselves advancing a charge on capitalism that lacked a sufficient number of dedicated fighters.[37]

One fascinating aspect of the cooperative brand of self-help is that it seems to have been "antiradical." Simply put: cooperativism is not socialism. Without doubt, the prevailing brand of capitalism would have been dramatically modified by concerns in the nation like Farmers' Mercantile and Elevator Company. Yet true radical advocates of economic change during the 1890s urged creation of public ownership of elevators and mills, usually by state governments. This eventually did occur, but only in a limited fashion when that political prairie fire, the Non-Partisan League, swept across North Dakota during the era of the First World War and brought a healthy dosage of agrarian socialism to the state in 1919.[38]

A rare insight into this cooperativism versus socialism response to depression-era conditions came from the pen of the editor of the *Co-operation,* a Denver mutualist newspaper. "I frankly know that the revolutionary spirit associated with state ownership is being dampened—certainly altered by the rapid expansion of the co-operative business." Still he expressed no grief. "To my way of seeing it, the co-operative operation is wholly workable. It brings positive and publically acceptable improvements for those who participate." Moreover, he took the opportunity to report a cardinal principal of cooperativism: "[It] is done with dispatch . . . without waiting until the [political] representatives come around to act."[39]

Perhaps an organic-type process was at work. Cooperatives conceivably became a starting point toward major change. Since they were devices that could be implemented outside the political process, they naturally occurred first. Then when the "people" captured the reins of government, socialism might well result. After all, those North Dakotans who gave rise to the Non-Partisan League initially tried the mutual approach and simply added public-owned facilities to their economic structure once they got power. Similarly, contemporaries contended that the years of depression forced individuals who heretofore showed little interest or understanding of group efforts to experience the value of cooperative action. A Louisiana timber worker and Socalist party organizer captured this process in a 1903 letter: "The cooperative zeal that swept the land in the recent years has made folks aware of what . . . socialism means [and] what it can do for them. . . ."[40]

While not an identical movement, the crusade for consumer-owned railroads duplicates much of the story of cooperative businesses. A "Let's-Build-Railroads-Now" program emerged during the hard times of the nineties that in its various forms offered the customary hope and relief from the ravages of hard times. But farmers' railroads also suggested a corrective, albeit nonradical, alternative to the incumbent economic structure of the transportation system, much as cooperatives did for merchandising.

# Farmers' Railroads

S the nation's first large business, the railroad industry established an enviable record for innovation. Whether spearheading uniform time zones, embracing standardized tools and structures, or demonstrating how to curb cutthroat competition through traffic pools, rail carriers pioneered a rich diversity of change following the Civil War. Yet not all industry triumphs brought public approval.[1]

With an arrogance characteristic of the "Gilded Age," railroad companies commonly abused consumers. Anti-industry feelings, therefore, developed over a variety of perceived evils. While service-related problems annoyed and even angered patrons, other grievances troubled them much more deeply. Watered stock, tax dodging, and rampant bribery worried many. But the foremost concern centered on rates, particularly freight charges. The conventional wisdom of the day held that carriers existed to plunder rather than to serve. The general populace, unfortunately, usually had no choice but to turn to the "iron horse" for its transportation needs. In most areas rails rather than waterways were the only effective means of shattering isolation. A Chicago merchant said it best: "Railroads are the magic carpets that bind the Republic. . . . [They] . . . are the only mode of dependable travel between most points."[2]

The experiences of Iowa rail users with shipping costs in the 1880s are typical. Reflecting grass-roots sentiment, the state's Board of Railroad Commissioners reported in 1886 that it was impossible to convince the average Hawkeye agrarian of the justice of prevailing conditions that forced him to give one boxcar of corn to pay the transportation bill of another to the Chicago market. And the board told of rate discrimination. "There is a great deal of general complaint [among farmers] because railways do charge from $60 to $80 from Western Iowa, when it is understood that cars from points still farther west are taken right by their door to some eastern point for considerably less." More than agricultural interests felt aggrieved; local businessmen demanded that the carriers "must make a car-load rate to apply to all the manufacturers and jobbers in Iowa, . . . or get ready for such a fight as they have never had on the prairies between the Mississippi and Missouri rivers before." As the influential *Iowa State Register* for August 24, 1887, succinctly put it: "Iowa is paying too large a freight bill."[3]

Since transportation costs remained high, the depression years of the 1890s understandably aggravated shipper resentment. "Our freight rates are the ruination of this country," snarled a North Dakota newspaper editor in 1896. Customers generally shared this point of view; but what could be done to control the railroad enterprise?[4]

The commonly proposed solutions took two principal forms. The famed Omaha Platform of 1892 revealed the radical approach. Specifically, the People's party argued: "We believe that the time has come when the railroad corporations will either own the people or the people must own the railroads." Public ownership theoretically ensured rate and service justice. The independent, proconsumer regulatory commission represented an alternative. This device seemed more obtainable than the Populist dream of a nationalized rail network for various agencies had already been established in some states and at the national level. Yet by the depression era commissions seemed wanting. Those that existed to regulate intrastate transportation proved nearly always to be weak and ineffective, while the federal Interstate Commerce Commission, launched in 1887, seemed little better. Observed H. T. Newcomb about the latter in the *Political Science Quarterly* nearly a decade after the Commission's founding:

> The Interstate Commerce law has mitigated but slightly, if at all, the evil of unjust discriminations between individuals; has in but few instances moderated to any important extent the relative injustice in the charges exacted for moving competing commodities; and has almost utterly failed to remedy the far more serious inequities in rate-making which operate to the disadvantage of towns, cities, or districts.[5]

Still a third possibility existed and received some support during the desperate days of the nineties. The so-called farmers' railroad was seen not only as a way to complement public regulation but also as a device to serve as either a substitute for government ownership or as a stopgap device until it occurred. Whatever the expectation, this novel type of railroad scheme grew up as another self-help method proposed to assist depression victims.

In its purest form on paper, a farmers' railroad was a consumer-launched business venture. Disgruntled shippers (or those who lacked adequate rail facilities) would incorporate the company, publicize organizational meetings, survey the route, and direct construction. Since capital would be scarce, farmers and townspeople—anyone who lived along the projected line—would be asked to donate right-of-way and to contribute their labor. (Often, for those who helped, company stock would be their immediate reward.) The available animal teams would shape the roadbed, and crossties ideally would be harvested from nearby stands of trees. When grading was completed and ties furnished, the infant road would be bonded to raise funds to purchase the cheapest suitable rail and rolling stock. The ultimate fate of the finished project usually remained flexible. Perhaps it might be sold or leased to a major trunk carrier with the agreed understanding that customers would receive the best possible rates and services. Or, more likely, the line would be operated indefinitely as a cooperative enterprise.


UNLIKE EITHER the community garden or the labor exchange, the precise origins of the farmers' railroad remain clouded. The concept of a cooperative or consumers' road unmistakably predates the Panic of 1893. One example is the Indianapolis-based People's Railroad of America.[6] Organized in 1883 to construct a double-track, narrow-gauge road from New York to San Francisco and from Chicago to New Orleans, this Bunyanesque undertaking was intended to offer "the little fellow the right to be a Drew or Gould . . . to build a railroad that would be free of plungers and one that would offer cheap, safe travel for all. . . ." This "Hit at Railroad Monopolies" would be a "mutual benefit association" with employees as the principal stockholders. While later discussion centered on constructing the line's first segment, the stretch from Indianapolis to the West coast, agitation fizzled within a year.[7]

Doubtlessly the most publicized plan prior to the depression was the Texas, Topolobampo, and Pacific Railroad. Conceived in the fertile mind of Albert K. Owen, a civil engineer turned communitarian, the utopian Credit Foncier Company began in 1885 to develop one of North America's greatest natural harbors, located on

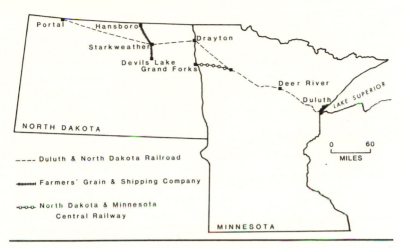

*The farmers' railroad movement on the Northern
Great Plains.*

the Gulf of California in the Mexican state of Siñaloa. Specifically, Owen sought to erect Pacific City "on the shores of Topolobampo and Ohuira Bays, upon a plan drawn from careful studies of the world's best improved cities and of the requirements of the new civilization to be developed." This grand community would be linked to the United States by a railroad that the colonists themselves planned to construct. As previously seen, Owen had devised a labor-check system to remunerate fellow workers; railroad builders supposedly would be paid in this fashion. Although Pacific City eventually reached a population of several hundred, an eight-mile irrigation ditch rather than a railroad occupied residents until the experiment's ultimate collapse.[8]

When hard times struck, a flurry of farmers' railroad agitation occurred. Proposals appeared widely. The heaviest concentration centered on the Great Plains where conditions were ideal: depressed populace and widespread railroad abuse. The representative plan was of modest length, usually 50 to 100 miles, although a few enthusiasts hatched spectacular schemes reminiscent of the People's Railroad of America. The American Pacific Railroad Company was undoubtedly the most gargantuan of the nineties. In an elegant pamphlet published in early 1897, backers told of their intention to construct a transcontinental trunk line that, together with branches, would constitute a network of over 7,000 miles. "It is a stupendous undertaking," was indeed no misstatement. But characteristically optimistic, the proponents concluded that "we believe it is practicable if pushed forward with energy according to plans laid down." Resembling the labor exchange episode especially, these self-help railroads took a variety of forms. Typically pragmatic, each effort seemed to adapt itself to specific needs.[9]

Nationally several major proposals took place before a type of farmers' railroad actually opened. The first important "people's" road plan of the 1890s was not a bona fide farmers' railroad at all. Yet it contained the essence of later dreams. Known officially as the Gulf and Inter-State Railway Company (G&I), and chartered by Kansas officials in early 1894, this grandiose proposition represents the most ambitious desires. As the corporate title implies, the road sought a terminal on the Gulf of Mexico, probably Galveston, and then planned to build a bifurcated system northward. One stem would reach into Manitoba, while another would end at Lake Superior. The former would traverse Texas, Indian Territory, Kansas, Nebraska, and the Dakotas; the latter would slice Arkansas, Missouri, Iowa, and Minnesota. This massive project would be a "second Illinois Central," a private carrier already correctly dubbed by some as the "wrong-way transcontinental."[10]

A cross section of interests backed the G&I. Generally, supporters came from the ranks of farmers, most of whom embraced the objectives of the Populists' Omaha Platform. To develop construction strategy, the road's prime mover, Alonzo Wardall, well known regionally for his advocacy of cooperative insurance and his organizing efforts for the Farmers Alliance, called together a "people's railroad convention" in Lincoln, Nebraska, on June 28-29, 1893. Termed a "pronounced success" by the *Dakota Ruralist,* the approximately fifty delegates from eight states and territories who gathered in the Cornhusker capital adopted a charter and, more important, outlined how to realize their vision. All agreed that the company was a fine idea. After all, said one representative, "The railroad trust must be overturned and rates slashed. Charges for which often nearly consume the entire value of the product as to leave no adequate reward either to the laborer who has produced it or the buyer who has shipped it."[11]

Without question, funding the G&I emerged as the chief problem. Proponents, nevertheless, formulated a multifaceted program to raise the thirty to fifty million dollars required for this stupendous undertaking. The firm would first of all issue six million dollars of nondividend-paying common stock. Communities along the projected routes were expected to acquire this paper, buying it through the sale of their own bonds. "Practically, this will be a donation to the company; but the donors will generally more than get their money back, directly, in taxes—to say nothing of incidental benefits." (This was a twist to the standard format for financing much of the country's railroads during the 1870s and 1880s; real-estate taxes, usually 5 percent of the value of assessed property, generated the funds for local subsidies.) Moreover, the G&I would issue twelve million dollars of preferred stock, likewise nondividend paying. Rather than being earmarked for municipalities, these securities were to be sold to sympathetic individuals. But unlike typical business transactions, the G&I would provide twenty-two five-dollar "transportation certificates" with each one hundred dollar lot of the paid-in preferred stock. When the system opened, these highly novel coupons would be accepted for railroad services. "[They] will be received in half payment for all kinds of business done by the company—a five-dollar certificate and five dollars in money paying for a ten-dollar [passenger] ticket or for that much freight." Not only would holders benefit from future reduction in transportation charges, but the road designed this paper to have a labor exchange–type function. "It is expected that these certificates will circulate as currency, to some extent, along the line of the road, when building. . . ." As one booster observed, "We can have our cake and eat it also—a railroad that will not ruin us but some immediate money for the people to use in the market-towns."[12]

The final two methods of fund raising for the G&I centered on bond sales. The road anticipated the issuance of income construction bonds that bore 5 percent interest. Most probably, state governments would acquire them; yet, like the so-called transportation certificates, backers expected that these instruments would also circulate as currency. And the G&I would float first mortgage bonds, not to exceed ten thousand dollars per mile and bearing not more than 5 percent interest. "Being the only lien on the road, they will be a choice investment and it is believed it will not be necessary to go east to sell them." Once more the expectation existed that public bodies would subscribe liberally.[13]

The G&I ultimately would become a public facility, thus fully in tune with the Populist sentiments of its backers. As mentioned, local government funds would purchase bonds initially. But once the carrier started, efforts would be made to have the various states in the service area assume the operation financially and operate it. Until that time, according to the proponents, the G&I's profits, if any, "shall be paid into the school fund of the several counties of the several states." The philosophy of the road's backers was to build it "not especially for the members of the company, but in the interest of humanity and for the benefit of the public at large."[14]

Labor also would profit when the G&I opened. In an era of drastic pay reductions and job cutbacks, the G&I expected to offer fair wages and to hire all necessary employees. Sympathetic to the newly launched American Railway Union, headed by Eugene V. Debs, the "Gulf to Canada" pike would encourage its workers to organize along industrial lines: "the trade-union idea has ceased to be useful or adequate . . . and the big union is the practical hope for the future." The statement was logically made that "We are forward-looking, for we offer a new deal to shippers and a new deal to workers."[15]

The desire to create an alternative rail network for much of the nation's midsection is understandable. The G&I, correctly labeled "a revolutionary railway," was envisioned as a wholly bootstrap project. It certainly made sense—times were hard, railroads repeatedly committed acts of corporate arrogance, and the People's party's presidential ticket had just experienced defeat. "Why not aid ourselves with our own [rail]road, for Government ownership is not about to come for some-time if ever," argued one Nebraskan. For that matter, tougher federal regulation was not anticipated.[16]

While vegetables, labor exchange checks, and cooperative concerns helped individuals, the G&I, if built, would likewise have greatly assisted the typical rail patron. But this self-help notion contained another dimension: "employment for tramps." Admittedly, aid for the jobless never emerged as the G&Is raison d'être; it was fundamentally a device to lower transportation charges. Still, the firm, resembling sister projects of the nineties, would provide this added benefit: putting to work hundreds of souls who desperately needed jobs. "Many folks will be able to earn much needed income as the road is under construction." At the least, those who would labor on the G&I "could earn stock for sweat." Farmers with their teams, especially, "would have a chance to increase their personal holdings." Naturally when placed in operation the G&I would emerge as an important regional employer; in the age of steam, railroads were highly labor intensive.[17]

Despite such an anticipatory build up, the G&I Railway never turned a wheel, although it sold some securities and conducted several track surveys. While the reasons for its failure are uncertain, the grandiose scope of the project undoubtedly crippled it. Noted a Kansas journalist in 1895, a year after interest in the G&I peaked, "The Gulf Route is needed . . . [but] the common people can never orchestrate this difficult proposition." And there seems to be at least one other consideration for the G&I's inability to succeed. A largely parallel private route, Arthur E. Stilwell's Kansas City, Pittsburg, and Gulf Railroad, was then in the process of laying steel from Kansas City to deep water; this road drove in the last spike on September 11, 1897, and the "straight as the crow flies" artery soon gave prairie shippers a valuable transportation alternative.[18]

The best known project comparable to the ill-fated G&I similarly sought to construct extensive mileage. Rather than a north-south route, this railroad planned to build on an east-west axis between the great transportation gateways of Chicago and Omaha. Midwestern Populists, mostly Iowans, launched the American Railway Company on May 13, 1896, when they filed the appropriate articles of incorporation with the Iowa Secretary of State.[19]

The G&I no doubt served as an inspiration and model. James T. R. Green of Des Moines, American Railway secretary, repeatedly used the agitation for the Gulf route as a positive sign that consumers, particularly farmers, wanted government or at least cooperative rail systems. The rhetoric commonly employed by proponents of this Iowa-based carrier echoed oft-repeated statements of the day. "People ownership of public services, like our planned-for American Ry. Co., is not only highly desirable, but inevitable for the simple reason that people cannot go on forever paying tribute to an idle, non-producing class." Even though Iowa and Illinois enjoyed superb rail connections, "rates in the states are altogether too high and the companies too powerful with the lawmakers." Moreover, "we need a climate that is hospitable to railroad labor where a schedule of wages is reasonable and the work duties fair and safe."[20]

Backers of the Omaha to Chicago route developed a less complicated method of financing. Estimating the railroad to cost five million dollars minimally (approximately five hundred miles at ten thousand dollars per mile), the firm would rely almost entirely on individual subscriptions. Potential patrons hopefully would purchase 500,000 shares at ten dollars each. The company would not seek state assistance, although individual communities along the projected line might acquire stock and donate real estate. Customary with this type of self-help effort, supporters unable to make cash investments could earn securities through donated labor.[21]

One imaginative feature of the G&I incorporated into the structure of the American Railway was the transportation certificate. Rather than providing these coupons at the time of the stock sale, the firm would distribute them to investors in lieu of cash dividends. As with the G&I, the scrip could be used for payment of all rail services. And the backers of the American Railway had another reason for endorsing certificates. A promotional broadside duly noted: "[A] motive of the . . . Company is to give better service (competition) in transportation then has hitherto been obtained. As a means of that end we believe that our transportation certificates . . . can be used to great advantage." The rationale was clear. If the people's company could haul "hogs and humans" virtually at cost between the gateways of Chicago and Omaha, competitors would be forced to slash rates and even to upgrade the quality of service.[22]

Although Iowa Populists embarked on a stock-sale campaign during the summer of 1896, they raised only a limited amount of funds. By autumn the possibilities of a trunk line paralleling the Chicago, Rock Island, and Pacific between Omaha and Chicago, through Des Moines, seemed dim. Undoubtedly this was due in large measure to the American Railway's projected route. While potential investors may have sympathized with the road's objectives, they probably recognized that it would produce redundant trackage. Several well-entrenched competing carriers already bound the two terminals. In addition to the Rock Island, the Chicago, Burlington, and Quincy; the Chicago, Milwaukee, and St. Paul; and the Chicago and North Western linked the gateways. And the Wabash also operated, although indirectly, between Omaha and Chicago.[23]

These conditions may explain why American Railway Company officials late in 1896 concocted another routing strategy. The new scheme was not only more plausible but far less costly. If the firm could span the 165 miles between Omaha and Hampton, Iowa, it could connect with the Chicago Great Western Railway (CGW) for direct access to Chicago. The CGW, created and run by the iconoclastic Alpheus Beede Stickney, correctly called the only midwestern railroad owner to appreciate shipper demands, seemed receptive to the cooperative road's intentions. For one thing, this trunk carrier, virtually alone in the industry, encouraged its several thousand employees to buy company stock. Moreover, repeatedly squeezed by hostile competitors, the CGW—namely Stickney himself—willingly made deals with other roads, real or "paper." Since the CGW lacked access to the Omaha gateway (it would enter the city on its own rails in 1903), the American Railway plans received thoughtful consideration.[24]

While the twilight days of the American Railway Company are unknown, the strong upswing in the regional economy on the eve of the Spanish-American War probably helped to dash the road's chances for success. Furthermore, the CGW decided to build into Omaha under its own banner. Perhaps if the backers of the American Railway had started earlier and selected the Hampton route initially, a triumph would have followed. Nevertheless, their efforts are testimony to the willingness among embattled souls to think big and attempt this self-help solution to a troublesome problem. It is understandable that Secretary Green sprinkled his public pronouncements with his favorite, albeit appropriate platitude, "God helps those who help themselves."[25]

Unlike the American Railway, the Duluth and North Dakota Railroad Company (D&ND) emerged as a self-help venture that held an especially bright promise. The classic farmers' railroad proposal, this carrier hoped to link northwestern North Dakota with Lake Superior. Rails would tie the two terminal communities, Portal, near the Canadian border in Burke County, North Dakota, and Duluth, Minnesota, a distance of about five hundred miles. The former offered a valuable connection with the Canadian Pacific and the latter was the premier western port of the Great Lakes, a city pushing hard to overtake the Twin Cities as the center of transportation and milling in the Upper Midwest. Differing from either the G&I or the American Railway, one individual, the remarkable "Farmer" Hines, formulated and single-handedly spearheaded the D&ND.[26]

David Wellington Hines (1863–1926) came from a background similar to those of his Dakota neighbors. Born on a hardscrabble farm in Simcoe County, Ontario, Canada, he received little formal education. When Hines attended school, "he was generally at the head of his class and was greatly praised by his teachers." Although briefly in the classroom, he successfully absorbed the era's ubiquitous self-help philosophy.[27] Hines learned an appropriate piece of popular poetry that he later claimed became "my motto":

> Once or twice though you should fail,
>      Try, Try Again
> If you would, at last prevail,
>      Try, Try, Again;
> If we strive, 'tis no disgrace,
> Though we may not win the race;
> What should you do in that case?
>      Try, Try, Again.[28]

In the mideighties, toward the end of the "Great Dakota Boom," young Hines, like hundreds of fellow Canadians, settled in Cavalier County. He selected a 160-acre farm site near the village of Hannah. A hard worker, Hines immediately hired himself out to earn the funds he would need to succeed as a farmer, and "he continued to work out most of the time for the next five years." Hines married a local girl and became a family man. Deeply religious, he served as a Methodist lay minister and when not preaching actively assisted the church as a Sunday school superintendent and teacher.[29]

The area press regularly praised David Hines for his solid citizenship. "A self-made man and a hustler of the true western type," concluded one editor. Yet a neighborhood journalist at the time of the farmers' railroad agitation described him as "nervous," while another went so far as to label him "crazy." To which Hines responded: "I am no Coxeyite, not a crank, but one of Cavalier County's most successful farmers, who has sacrificed everything but wife, life and religion for to benefit our country by getting a direct line of railroad from Duluth to Portal, in opposition to the Great Northern."[30]

Residents of the Upper Plains traditionally demonstrated an innovative flare for solving their severe transportation problems. Since inadequate outlets historically plagued the region, settlers experimented with two methods before the ultimate triumph of the railroad. Shipper-owned steamboats plied the shallow and snag-infested waters of the Red River of the North between the Dakota and Minnesota ports and Winnipeg before the vessels of James J. Hill's Red River Transportation Company captured much of the traffic in the mid-1870s. Earlier these prairie pioneers developed a unique form of surface transport, the "Red River cart." Hundreds of these oxen-drawn vehicles with their huge, squeaking wooden wheels hauled up to 800 pounds of cargo between the Red River valley and the Twin Cities. And the area's quest for better transportation would likewise be reflected in farmers' railroads.[31]

The precise origins of the D&ND are obscure. However, "Farmer" Hines wrote in 1894 that the probable beginnings occurred during the previous year. He and several fellow agrarians apparently came in contact with a nearby Rolette County farmer named Becker, who lived in the vicinity of Rolla. "Becker said we ought to organize a railroad company and get our charter, do some work and then some company would buy us out and go on with the construction of the road."[32]

The Becker suggestion struck a responsive chord. Not only were Dakotans in the throes of severe agricultural depression ("Twenty miles to water; forty miles to wood! We're leaving North Dakota and we're leaving her for good!"), but transportation problems abounded. Neither river travel (the Red flowed in the wrong direction for the principal American markets) nor the now largely forgotten carts would suffice. Railroads were the answer. But certain sections of the upper two tiers of counties lacked adequate rail outlets; where flanged wheels existed, costs seemed both prohibitive and grossly unfair. Few residents perceived Hill's Great Northern Railway, the steam road that had a lock on most of the region's service, to be the consumer's friend. Observed a Cavalier County wheat producer,

> We [farmers] can bear a great many things, but there are some things that we won't stand much longer. One of them is paying double freight rates. Railroad companies get about half of our money every year; in fact, we are their slaves. We furnish everything and give them half the crop. . . . We have stuck to Jim Hill's road long enough.[33]

A seismograph of public tremors, Hines began to lay the groundwork for a company that would be truly a farmers' railroad. Before he and his supporters filed the official papers of incorporation for the D&ND with the secretary of state in Bismarck on August 20, 1894, he turned newspaper editor. On June 18 Hines published the maiden issue of a weekly organ he fittingly named the *Farmer's Railroad*. Initially headquartered in Cavalier, he subsequently moved operations to another Pembina County community, Drayton, that abutted the North Dakota-Minnesota border.[34]

The *Farmer's Railroad* made sense. As backer Warren Sheaf explained, "A paper is as necessary in building a railroad as in building up a town.'' Indeed, the overall impact of this publication should not be ignored or even minimized. Lawrence Goodwyn has cogently argued in his monumental work on Populism that ''Insurgent movements are not the product of 'hard times,' they are the product of insurgent cultures.'' Conceivably, the columns of this modest four-page tract created a milieu much more conducive to a self-help railroad than the environments associated with similar projects. For more than two years the *Farmer's Railroad* fired its readership's hatred of monopolies, particularly Hill's Great Northern, and argued for the cooperative alternative to the ''trustification'' of American life. At the least, the publication sought to create one example of the ideal common carrier, the D&ND. Together with Hines's own powerful, even charismatic personality and persuasive oratory, the *Farmer's Railroad* generated an intensity of opinion that simply never existed with the efforts to build either the G&I or the American Railway. ''Through his weekly sheets 'Farmer' Hines had made these farmers crazy for the scheme,'' remarked a Minneapolis reporter.

> They are full of that redhot desire to see this thing through for he keeps hounding them. . . . he does this by hitting them every week in that little paper and at his [railroad] convention camp meetings. . . . The farmers are convinced that they must work out their own salvation through the D&ND.[35]

Farmer Hines knew the five-hundred-mile pike could be constructed. ''We have always been told that it takes an awful lot of money to build a railroad, but we wish to inform our readers that after all a great deal can be done with a very little money.'' And sounding like a Methodist preacher, he added: ''If we have lots of faith, I am sure it is as good as lots of money . . . a man can do wonders with a peck of faith and a pint of money.'' From a ''nuts and bolts'' standpoint, Hines realistically estimated that the cost of building and equipping the D&ND would be low, only about eight thousand dollars per mile since the firm specified only minimal construction standards (''two rails on a mudbank''). Most of this could be raised by exchanging work for company stock, and as he said, ''None of us will feel any poorer for it.''[36]

While officially chartered, the D&ND continued for some time to remain solely on paper and in the minds of Farmer Hines and his hundreds of supporters. Not until 1896 did the road take on tangible dimensions, and by then construction plans had been significantly altered. Just as American Railway Company backers chopped their line's projected mileage by nearly two-thirds, Hines cut his road by approximately the same amount. The carrier would now run in an easterly direction for 166 miles from Drayton, in the heart of the Red River valley, to Deer River, Minnesota. This community offered an interchange connection with the Minneapolis, St. Paul, and Sault Ste. Marie Railway (Soo Line) and supposedly "the best of freight rates . . . to Duluth."[37]

In a widely reprinted "Questions Asked and Answered" column from the *Farmer's Railroad,* Hines provided the exact details of construction for the truncated D&ND:

> *Q. When and where are you going to commence laying track on the farmers' road?*
> A. We expect to commence next June at Deer River [Minnesota], which is 108 miles from Duluth and is the terminus of the . . . Soo line.
> *Q. Will the Soo line make connection with the farmers' road?*
> A. Yes. . . .
> *Q. Is it a hard country [from Deer River to Red River, North Dakota] to build through, and will it contribute much freight to your road?*
> A. The first 70 miles from Deer River to Red Lake [Falls] is solid timber, mostly pine, cedar, tamarack, birch and maple, and as our line runs right along the divide or water shed of Minnesota, it is principally level, with neither rocks or hills, and from Red Lake [Falls] to Red River it is so level that the ties could be laid right on the prairie, which is the finest farming land in the State. Our cars would all be loaded with lumber and wood coming west, and grain going east.
> *Q. What will new rails with spikes and connecting bars cost laid down at Deer River?*
> A. $3,165 per mile. . . .
> *Q. How can you get the money?*
> A. By bonding our road-bed and ties.
> *Q. What will you do for rolling stock?*
> A. As a great many other roads do, rent it until we are able to buy on time.
> *Q. What do cars and engines cost?*
> A. Box cars are made in Duluth, and are worth $408 each; engines from $6,000 to $9,000; passenger coaches from $2,000 to $3,500.
> *Q. How much can freight rates be reduced on the farmers' road?*

A. One-half, and still make large profits.
Q. *Does the company think they will get the road built?*
A. They don't think anything about it—they know it.
Q. *How do they know it?*
A. They know it because it's one of the most feasible routes of a road in  America. Just think of it, we grow now over 100,000,000 bushels of grain, which all goes a round about way to market, and all our lumber, wood, coal, in fact everything comes and goes the same way. There are over 300,000 people who will be directly benefited by the road. They are paying more money each year in extortionate freight rates than would build the road, and they know it, and are just waiting for some good, honest men to take the lead and they are all ready to follow, and we know it.[38]

As a farmers' railroad project, the D&ND flopped. Although teams of workers harvested thousands of hardwood ties from the Minnesota forests and shaped several miles of grade near Drayton, the road never progressed any farther. Yet agitation for the D&ND produced positive results. The progress of the Hines scheme prompted the Great Northern during the grain-shipping season of 1895 to slash wheat rates on both the Langdon and Cavalier branches, the two GN lines that served northeast North Dakota. Moreover, James J. Hill conceded that the route from the Red River valley to Duluth was an excellent one. Within a few years after the farmers' railroad died, Great Northern freight and passenger trains rumbled the 270 miles between Crookston, Minnesota (sixty miles southeast of Drayton), and Duluth. This latter event did not anger David Hines.  Reported the *Grand Forks Daily Herald* in January 1900: "The failure of his scheme to build a road to Duluth has been offset by a transportation line that furnishes all that can be desired, and he is content."[39]

Still, "Farmer" Hines knew that he had a good idea. Although he left North Dakota for his native Canada early in the century, he made another attempt at launching a self-help railroad. Hines became the driving force behind the Farmer's Railway Company, organized in 1909. Initially, this firm planned to tie Hudson Bay with the United States in the vicinity of Plentywood, Montana, but Hines and his farmer associates soon settled on bridging the fifty miles between the Saskatchewan communities of Melfort and Humboldt. Actually, the story of this second venture largely duplicates the first. Area agrarians graded about five miles of roadbed before the project collapsed; and an entrenched road, the Canadian Pacific, subsequently completed the work.[40]

The farmers' railroad movement on the Upper Great Plains is not limited solely to David Wellington Hines and the D&ND. While he labored mightily for his own road, Hines encouraged others to seek cooperatively built carriers. Independent of the D&ND was the North Dakota and Minnesota Central Railway. Begun in January 1896, this self-help railroad sought to connect the counties of Grand Forks, North Dakota, and Polk, Minnesota, with the Hines road in west-central Minnesota. Although this company proved to be totally "hot-air," another Farmer Hines-inspired venture, the Farmers' Grain and Shipping Company, actually materialized.[41]

THE LONE FARMERS' railroad triumph of the 1890s originated out of a series of public meetings held in Devils Lake, North Dakota, and the surrounding countryside during the winter of 1895–1896. Ramsey County citizens resented those "evil acts of the Hill Road" and longed for relief. "If we are to get transportation satisfaction," wrote one resident to Hines, "then the boot-strap rail-road that you are making so popular is just the ticket."[42]

Not until after the turn of the century did the Farmers' Grain

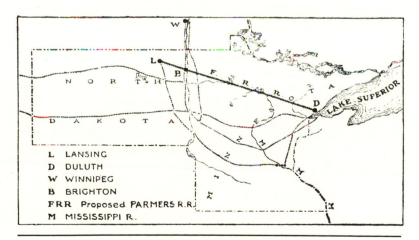

*Although "Lansing" and "Brighton" are ficti-
tious town names, this map, which accompanied
the largely accurate 1899* McClure's Magazine *account of the Hines farmers' railroad, correctly indicates the proposed route of the ill-fated project.*

and Shipping Company evolve into a bona fide carrier. The future road received its greatest boost from a wealthy local wheat grower, Joseph M. Kelly, "one who operates on a big scale and deals in big projects." Unlike Farmer Hines, who earned the credentials of an advanced reformer, Kelly was no radical. He was instead a hard-nosed agribusinessman concerned with enhancing his income and the value of his real estate. "The Colonel [Kelly] is not inspired with the longing to help his other fellow farmers," observed a local Hines supporter. "He is in the railroad business to get a dependable outlet for his crops, nothing more and nothing less."[43]

Dreams started to become reality in April 1900 when Kelly and Rasmus Sorenson, another prosperous farmer, and John W. Maher, a Devils Lake attorney, launched a subscription drive for what they called the Devils Lake and Northern Railway Company. Their idea was to push a rail line in a northerly direction into a largely set-tled inland region of Ramsey County and perhaps ultimately to the international boundary or even on into Manitoba. Such a road would "traverse as fine a section of farming country as the sun ever shown on." Kelly and his associates did not incorporate their proj-ect; rather, it remained for the next two years merely an association of individuals who desired what they knew to be the only dependa-ble means of transportation—a railroad. Scores of agrarians agreed to help. Offers came for donations of right-of-way parcels and of animal and human muscle power; cash, too, trickled into Maher's Devils Lake office.[44]

Dirt flew on the initial section of the farmers' road during the summer of 1900. But for two years wet weather badly hampered the project. Then in 1902 the final several miles of grading were fin-ished, and residents completed the track installation. On September 15 the first train chugged into the newly built village of Stark-weather, twenty-three and one-half miles north of Devils Lake. Im-mediately, the company's lone locomotive picked up cars bulging with the season's grain crop for the Twin Cities marketplace.[45]

Since volunteer labor aided the Devils Lake and Northern con-siderably, its actual cost was modest. The total price was about twelve thousand dollars per mile. Two-thirds accrued from the sale of stock to area farmers. The remaining four thousand dollars per mile came from the proceeds of a bond sale.[46]

By the fall of 1902, the Kelly people believed that they should officially incorporate. They therefore filed a petition of organiza-tion with the North Dakota secretary of state; soon a charter was is-sued for what was called the Farmers' Grain and Shipping Company (FG&SCo). According to Article Two, the firm's principal purpose was "to handle, ship, and transport, by any power or method, grain, livestock and other property." Technically, the line lacked the status of a regular railroad. Kelly, the company president, made it clear to public officials that he wanted a "general business concern" and not a common carrier. The former status, Kelly told supporters, would keep the railroad commission from forcing the pike to remain open during the harsh winter months when such operations could become exceedingly expensive. After all, its raison d'être was grain hauling at harvest time.[47]

The change from the voluntary Devils Lake and Northern to the incorporated FG&SCo was not the brainstorm of Joseph Kelly or, for that matter, of any Ramsey County plowman. It came from the fertile mind of James J. Hill. The clever president of the Great Northern courted Kelly and encouraged him to push for the farmers' road, one that the "Empire Builder" expected to be a friendly feeder and a source of modest income. The Great Northern head probably viewed the incorporation strategy as an experiment. If it worked, the plan might have further applications. Hill not only suggested the noncommon carrier idea; he directed a company attorney to prepare the necessary legal papers.[48]

The closeness between the mighty Great Northern and the tiny FG&SCo was seen in other ways. At the time of construction, the Great Northern supplied building materials, often at cost and on credit, and it either leased or sold the necessary rolling stock. When the FG&SCo attempted to place its financial house in good order in 1903, the Great Northern accepted its gold bonds. This involvement with the Kelly road would soon become even more extensive.[49]

During the autumn of 1904 President Kelly and Attorney Maher traveled to St. Paul to visit Great Northern officials. They wanted to extend their road thirty miles to the northwest in order to tap additional areas that lacked adequate shipping facilities. The Hill firm could help. They hoped it would make construction supplies available at low cost and, more important, acquire FG&SCo securities. The Great Northern agreed.[50]

Work on the so-called Starkweather-Rock Lake Extension began in late 1904 and accelerated after the winter snows melted. The graders completed their labors in early August 1905, and soon a mammoth track-laying machine arrived. The line opened for revenue service on September 27. Unlike the original section, a commercial railroad builder speedily built the road. The financial ar-

rangements differed as well. The stocks and bonds Kelly gave the
contractor were purchased by the Great Northern, a transaction
that significantly increased its control over the fifty-four mile
shortline.[51]

The construction crews did not rest after they hammered the
last spike at Rock Lake. They quickly graded a thirteen-mile line to
the northwest that passed through the new townsite of Ellsberry
and terminated at another raw prairie village, Hansboro, a Towner
County community named in honor of United States Senator Henry C. Hansbrough. Within days workers laid the ties and installed
the steel.[52]

The dedication of Hansboro on November 5, 1905, was a gala
affair. Senator Hansbrough fittingly gave the principal address. He
complimented the road's backers for "their courageous efforts
throughout the several years of trials and tribulations that beset the
enterprise during its earlier history," and he regarded the line's
completion "as little less than marvelous." Concluded the senator,
"It was an achievement that has no parallel anywhere, and Messrs.
Kelly, Sorenson, and the farmers who have stood by them, deserve
the greatest credit for what they have done."[53]

Whether Senator Hansbrough knew the full story of the Farmers' Railroad's relationship with the Great Northern is uncertain.
Perhaps he was aware that the last thirteen miles from Rock Lake
to his namesake town were not officially trackage of the FG&SCo,
but belonged to the Brandon, Devils Lake & Southern (BDL&S), a
Great Northern satellite. What he said in his dedicatory speech simply reflected the popularly held notion that the Kelly road was *independent,* owned and operated by Ramsey and Towner county
transportation consumers. Yet by the time of the senator's speech
the Great Northern controlled the FG&SCo. Not only did the Hill
road own most of the funded debt, but it held 4,841 of the carrier's
8,000 shares of common stock. Even though the Great Northern
quickly leased the Brandon road to the Kelly people, it subsequently sold the Farmers' Railroad securities to the BDL&S, thus making
the FG&SCo a captive of a Great Northern affiliate.[54]

Domination of the FG&SCo offered the Great Northern numerous benefits. Indeed, this corporate relationship seemed better
than the two alternatives: an independent road that might be gobbled up by a rival carrier—perhaps the expansionistic Soo—or a
traditional branch line. The most candid explanation of the value
of having the Kelly pike as a corporate captive came from Great
Northern President Carl R. Gray. In a 1912 letter he argued that

"Aside from the fact that they [Farmers' Railroad officials] can unquestionably operate one of these little lines more economically than we can, there is a bigger question involved; that of having such men interested in railroad operations at all." As he noted, "I have found that when so interested they are the most potent influence against unfair legislation."[55]

Thus the Great Northern could literally have its cake and enjoy every tasty morsel. Even after the Soo opened its "Wheat Line" from Thief River Falls, Minnesota, to Kenmare, North Dakota, in 1905, which crossed the Farmers' Railroad at Olmstead and ran the Fordville-Drake route through Devils Lake seven years later, the Great Northern got virtually all the traffic generated by the Kelly road (grain and some livestock) and it delivered most of the inbound cars. Without a doubt, the FG&SCo's operating costs were lower than a comparable branch. Nonunion, skeleton crews shuttled the equipment over the "plug" line. Passenger, mail, and express service was usually part of a daily-except-Sunday "mixed" train. Since the firm gave the illusion of being free, demands by online patrons for better "varnish" were few; costly regular passenger trains were therefore avoided.[56]

By having the Devils Lake–Hansboro line under the banner of the FG&SCo, the regulatory milieu generally remained favorable. Annual tax bills in particular stayed modest. For most of its corporate existence, the road was assessed at a lower per-mile rate than any branch of the Great Northern, Milwaukee, Northern Pacific, or Soo in the state. The reason for this pro-FG&SCo policy is directly related to President Gray's observation that a captive firm found exemption from hostile legislation. Undeniably, the presence of what citizens perceived to be the independent, locally owned farmers' carrier translated into favorable considerations from politicians.[57]

The Great Northern did not garner all of the advantages of having control of the FG&SCo. In addition, Ramsey and Towner county folks benefited. For one thing, if the Great Northern had not provided financial assistance, the line might never have been built or at least not through its ultimate service region. Moreover, it had the advantages of personal, hometown management. Directors of the FG&SCo, for instance, gave independent grain buyers the first choice in elevator locations, and they continually "encouraged this class of grain dealers." This, naturally, reflected a popular farmer sentiment. And apparently freight service was good; few patron complaints exist. The Great Northern also emerged as a dependable supplier of quality rolling stock. Whether an engine or a caboose, the FG&SCo usually got what it wanted at reasonable, often bargain-basement prices. After all, "it is to our interest to have the road operated as economically and as efficiently as possible," explained a Great Northern official.[58]

But there surely would have been greater advantages if the Kelly operation had been truly a model farmers' railroad. Granted, the Great Northern treated the Devils Lake–Hansboro property with a certain amount of kindness; it was in the steam giant's best interest to do so. Patrons, however, never got their expected rate reductions. The average tariff charges equalled that on comparable trackage. Observed a shipper in 1909, "We have been forced to make a trade-off—good service with the G.N. for rather steep rates." Admittedly, extant records reveal that the farmers' road under Great Northern control was no stupendous money-maker, but the profits generated during its first quarter-century of operations might instead have been passed on to consumers in the form of reduced charges.[59]

If the FG&SCo had maintained a bona fide farmers' railroad status, the carrier's overall financial health might have been considerably better. In some ways disaster struck in 1905. Backers of the Soo Line correctly perceived the Kelly road as an instrument of Great Northern strategy. As a response the Soo built a branch from its "Wheat Line" at Egeland, near Olmstead, to Armourdale, that closely paralleled the FG&SCo and the BDL&S for more than twenty miles. The Soo sought to demonstrate to the Hill people that "This is a vast territory and it is rather unreasonable to expect that any one Railway Company can control the same." The correspondence of Soo Line General Manager Edmund Pennington reveals that if the FG&SCo had been free of Great Northern domination and willing to divert some traffic to his road, the Soo would never have penetrated the Olmstead-Hansboro region. The end result, understandably, was that the Armourdale branch damaged severely the income picture from the Kelly road's north end.[60]

Not only might have this Soo competitor been avoided, but a "Hines-like" operation conceivably could have been profitably pushed into nearby Killarney, Manitoba, approximately twenty miles northwest of Hansboro. Such an extension would have generated considerable on-line traffic and would have provided a key interchange at Killarney with the Canadian Pacific for Winnipeg, the West Coast, and other outlets. The Killarney Board of Trade and the Killarney Grain Growers Association eagerly backed the extension. But Joseph Kelly, the Great Northern's marionette in Devils

Lake, balked at the notion, and St. Paul officials said no to the Canadians. The potential benefits of a farmers' railroad were not to be. The FG&SCo remained a captive corporation until 1945, when it lost its corporate identity and became just another Great Northern branchline.[61]

The reasons for the farmers' railroad movement achieving its best record in North Dakota are open to speculation. Perhaps the economic environment served as the principal explanation for agitation and action. But another significant factor may exist. One student of populism, James Turner, contends that these uplifters mostly inhabited the "fringe of the dominant society." Indeed, North Dakota was such a place. The vast majority of North Dakota plowmen, at least those in areas that boosted the D&ND and the FG&SCo, lived in relative seclusion from the larger society. A sense of loneliness and disconnectedness possibly energized activities. Thus the Turner statement that "isolation breeds a political culture [in this case a self-help radicalism] at odds with the mainstream of political habits and attitudes" is worthy of consideration.[62]

THE URGE to lash out at transportation shortcomings took forms other than steam railroads. Self-help is nicely represented in agitation for wagon roads and electric interurban railways. While the Jacob S. Coxey–inspired crusade to have the federal government finance highway construction is not a genuine bootstrap example since it relied on the political process, the obscure "iron-road" notion of the mid-1890s represents a twist to the farmers' railroad concept.[63]

Apparently few, if any, iron roads appeared. Still, the idea was intriguing. One broadside, prepared by an Ohio workers' group, partially explains the concept:

> Why would not plates of iron 6 or 8 inches wide be laid on solid dirt roads, filled in with gravel to prevent slush and mud and for the horses to travel upon? These iron plates might be stayed every 10 or 12 feet to keep them in place. This plan would employ idle labor and would be the source of a great deal of comfort besides saving the public a great deal more than it costs in a few years' use. . . . Buggies, wagons and the immensely popular bicycles could roll smoothly to their destinations.[64]

The fundamentals also included flexible financing. Although local governments would probably enter the iron-road business (just as they did during the heyday of the "Good Roads" movement of the 1910s and 1920s), consumer-owned companies also might emerge. Whether public or private, construction bonds would be issued and a user's tax would likely be levied to liquidate the debt and to maintain the throughways. The scheme obviously resembles early tollways; ones that frequently employed a similar type of construction—the log corduroy. In a fashion highly reminiscent of the farmers' railroads, these iron roads would be "a great assistance in employing the out-of-work and providing an alternative to the steam carriers." Both the short and long-term objectives of the self-help impulse might then be conveniently incorporated into this imaginative transportation form.[65]

A better concept was the electric interurban. This new travel method became possible through major technological developments in the 1880s. Perhaps the pivotal breakthrough came in 1887 when Frank Julian Sprague, a recent graduate of the United States Naval Academy and a man intrigued with the commercial possibilities of electricity, succeeded in electrifying the Richmond (Virginia) Union Passenger Railway. Sprague's triumph set a pattern for a transportation revolution, and by the early nineties, additional research demonstrated the feasibility of long-range electric railway construction. Starting with a seven-mile "juice" line between Newark and Granville, Ohio, in 1889, "interurban" roads sprouted rapidly. By the eve of the Spanish-American War several score of firms claimed a total of nearly a thousand miles nationwide.[66]

The electric interurban was ideally suited for the self-help proponent. Most of all, this transportation device could easily penetrate an area that had inadequate steam competition or no rail service at all due largely to lower overall construction expenses. Most builders never designed their electric roads to duplicate the exacting standards employed on the major steam routes; branch lines became their models. The typical interurban of the day was modest in length, usually only twenty-five to thirty miles long. This factor further cut start-up and maintenance costs. And from an operating point of view, the potential for success seemed high. When compared to steam, electric equipment was cheaper. Traction cars and locomotives contained fewer moving parts than did the iron horse; they sported a much simpler and hence more easily repairable design. Electric rolling stock needed neither coal, water, fires to be banked, nor ashes to be removed; therefore firemen were not necessary. Crew sizes generally were much smaller for interurbans—only a motorman and conductor—rather than the four or five employ-ees required for a similar steam train.[67]

Compressed air claimed additional advantages over steam. Unquestionably, interurbans offered the public clean and conveni-ent service. Unlike the steam locomotive, the electric car boasted "no cinders, no dirt, no dust, no smoke." Electric roads operated with greater frequency than traditional ones; passenger movements often ran on hourly or semihourly schedules. These units stopped virtually anywhere, while steam-train "varnish" commonly made only several daily trips, pausing at a limited number of points. Elec-tric roads, moreover, could provide dependable service—compara-ble to their steam rivals. In an era when horse-drawn vehicles trav-eled over primitive roads repeatedly made impassible by the vaga-ries of weather, sleek interurban cars held an understandable at-traction.[68]

The extent of commitment by self-helpers during the depres-sion to cooperative interurban construction is unclear. Based on re-form-oriented publications and electric railway industry organs, at least a dozen or so such attempts occurred. Unlike the bulk of farmers' steam railroad schemes, electric ones were centered in the more heavily populated areas. The interurban of the 1890s lacked the capabilities for extensive length. Therefore this type of carrier was either suited as a short feeder for a conventional line or the link between communities in well-settled sections.[69]

By World War I Ohio emerged as the heartland of the electric interurban. Its electric mileage of 2,798 made the state's interurban map resemble a plate of wet spaghetti. This traction explosion is ex-plained by the state's heavy population density, characterized by numerous medium-sized cities and towns and a vast number of rural villages. While interurban fever badly infected residents after the turn of the century when general prosperity reigned, both "pa-per" and "real" roads appeared during the nineties. Even though Ohio agrarians escaped much of the suffering of the depression, they were not immune to railroad abuse. Admittedly, the local steam rail network offered greater competition than North Dako-ta's, for example, but as the *Breeder's Gazette* mentioned in 1895, "Farmers in Ohio . . . seem upset about the railroads and for good reason. Certain short-haul charges are exorbitant; they exceed the bounds of fairness and reason. . . . This comes at a particularly bad time." This agricultural journal also related a general unhap-piness with the quality of service provided by the steam carriers.

"Cars are often dirty . . . many are completely worn-out, and
sometimes the trains arrive hours late."[70]

This milieu understandably sparked agitation for relief. While
some Ohioans contemplated a traditional farmers' railroad, electric
railways gained a greater popularity. Efforts to span the forty miles
between Fremont and Toledo demonstrate the electric option. In
1896 Sandusky, Ottawa, and Wood County farmers began talk of
an electric road through their home localities. Inspired by the success of the neighboring Sandusky, Milan and Norwalk Railway's
seventeen-mile traction system that opened in 1893 (but constructed
through conventional financing), these agrarians proposed a line
that would be "paid for by the labors of the people." While individuals could make money commitments, the strategy adopted was
for those who owned land that abutted the survey not only to donate the right-of-way but to build the grade themselves. In both
cases stock would be issued to contributors. When the roadbed had
been readied, the firm planned to float bonds on the improvements
to pay for the track, trolley overhead, and the necessary pieces of
rolling stock. The anticipated passenger and freight (l.c.l.) tariffs
would be reasonable ("We will ruin the Lake Shore & Michigan
Southern's [steam competitor] business!"), with special considerations extended to individuals who aided construction. The plan
called for paying the track and overhead installers (farmers, townspeople, and the like) with stock or a combination of certificates and
cash.[71]

Resembling so many self-help transportation propositions, the
Fremont-Toledo traction company failed to take tangible shape for
mostly unknown reasons. Likely the financial burdens were too
great, for this was a time when capitalists generally had retrenched
and were themselves struggling to regroup. Perhaps a few entrepre-
neurs—in the tradition of Col. Joseph M. Kelly—grasped the great
potentials of an interurban based instead on a traditional business
structure. They could invest their capital and then reap personally
handsome windfalls. And that is what happened. The privately
funded Toldeo, Fremont and Norwalk Railway opened its sixty-
five-mile line between the communities of its corporate title in
1901. Soon the powerful Everett-Moore traction syndicate stepped
in and used this route as a link for its Cleveland to Toledo Lake
Shore Electric Railway, one of the nation's largest and most important electric roads. This scenario remarkably resembles the fate of
the FG&SCo.[72]

Even though the annals of interurban history reveal few carriers that ever attempted to follow the farmers' railroad blueprint, two elements of this self-help idea enjoyed widespread application. Nearly universal was the practice of real-estate donation. The reason is easily explained. Farmers especially wanted the economic advantages of electric roads and the overall freedom they could provide. Interurban companies often made it possible for potential patrons to earn stock through an exchange of labor. For example, Iowa's little Albia Interurban Railway Company employed this fund-raising method. In 1907–1908, when the firm was building its seven-mile line between Albia, the Monroe County seat, and the coal camp of Hiteman, it asked neighboring farmers and miners to assist in the construction and to accept both specie and stock for their labors. They agreed, and the road was completed.[73]

PLANS FOR FARMERS' RAILROADS contained an assumption that community gardens and labor exchanges consistently lacked but that was common to cooperative stores: they would be permanent. While potato patch advocates sought to fill empty bellies until the economic crisis passed and De Bernardi followers similarly adopted a scheme that most thought ephemeral, self-help railroad enthusiasts expected lasting institutions. As such, this particular illustration of uplift might be thought of as a serious challenge to the economic status quo. Like cooperative enterprises, the farmers' railroad movement was not a blueprint for state socialism, yet its intense cooperative spirit questioned prevailing forms of finance capitalism. "We will redirect the character of transportation," editorialized the *Farmer's Railroad*. "Ultimately the Goulds, Hills, and Harimans [*sic*] will be walking the streets and not riding the rails."[74]

Another important difference existed among farmers' railroads and gardens, exchanges and, to a degree, cooperative stores. Self-help transportation builders realized that their facilities could not offer immediate relief; the unemployed could not be put to work rapidly—railroads demanded years, not the weeks or months required for the other plans. Although if actually launched, self-help carriers might very well assist the out-of-work, and in large numbers. Moreover, they could provide favorable worker environments. While the farmers' railroad drive did virtually nothing to improve the unemployment picture, it, like related notions, gave hope to many who had lost faith in contemporary politics and perhaps in America itself. One North Dakotan said it best: the farmers' railroad was "a cheerful, uplifting experience."[75]

There is no way of knowing if the farmers' railroad movement significantly affected transportation reform. Directly, it probably did not. The occurrence, for example, of the D&ND scheme causing some rate adjustments by the Great Northern and the eventual construction of much of the Hines line, albeit by James J. Hill, held local importance; the national impact, beyond the rays of hope the crusade cast, was minimal at best. When a farmers' railroad at last appeared early in the twentieth century, it turned out to be simply the captive of a powerful corporation.

Although the relationship between self-help railroad agitation and subsequent Progressive era triumphs of strengthened state and federal regulatory controls is fuzzy, the former likely sustained, even promoted, an atmosphere conducive to the latter's accomplishments. More tangible, the interurban mania that swept much of the nation during the early years of the century and ultimately created more than fifteen thousand miles of electric trackage by 1915, produced in numerous localities a competitive, more favorable environment for consumers. And this form of intercity transportation, as seen, contained a strong self-help flavor.

The tumultuous nineties witnessed still another self-help phenomenon—intentional communities. Here, again, as with the drive for farmers' railroads, emerged the common elements of hope, pragmatism, and even radicalism. Indeed, these colonies might be considered the ultimate self-improving efforts.

# *Intentional Communities*

HE economic disaster that befell America during the nineties triggered an intense interest in the possibilities of creating utopia. Thousands of "forward looking" individuals, part of a new communitarianism, sought to build colonies that offered a haven for depression victims and models for what the nation might ideally become. Their efforts stand as classic self-help experiments, ones sought through careful, group initiative.

The "intentional" or specially designed community offered the unemployed unusual, even unique, opportunities. In this controlled environment, removed from the restraints and complexities of traditional society, full attention could be given to those down on their luck but willing to assist themselves. The mutually supportive nature of such an atmosphere presumably could inspire hope and the determination to succeed. An intentional community thus could be, in the words of an Iowa utopist, "a place to begin anew."[1]

The dominant thrust of utopian thought and action between 1893 and 1897 differed dramatically from the country's long communitarian tradition. These "new breeds" can be called "pragmatists," while conventional dreamers best sport labels of "cooperativists" and "charismatic perfectionists." The three categories are worthy of discussion.

Cooperativists, secular in composition like the pragmatists, expressed an essentially nonmodernist world vision. These utopists emphasized economic cooperation based on primitive cottage industries; they utterly rejected complex technology, root and branch. And they expressed only limited interest in political matters. Cooperativists typically saw their communities as ordered environments where predatory habits developed in cities could be effectively eliminated; where the bonds of family and marriage would be strengthened; and where conditions for moral growth would exist. The cooperativists did not originate in the 1890s; rather they had been part of the utopian scene for decades. The principal body flourished in the aftermath of the Panic of 1837—followers of the French reformer and communitarian Charles Fourier and his leading American disciple, Albert Brisbane. These so-called Associationists sought to achieve the good life by embracing the notions of agricultural self-sufficiency and rejecting large industry for craft-type workshops. In the same vein, the cooperativist view persisted into the twentieth century. The postindustrial agrarianism and "low-tech" philosophies of Harry Kelly and Austin Tappan Wright illustrate this continuum.[2]

However, the antebellum phalanxes of Fourier-Brisbane, resembling a few similarly structured experiments of the 1870s, foreshadowed the new order of the nineties. Even though the cooperativists staunchly resisted the technological advance of society, they perceived their colonies partially as sanctuaries for the economically troubled. "We are a shelter for the victims of the great financial misfortunes," remarked a member of the Iowa Pioneer Phalanx in 1844. "We provide the helping-hand for those souls willing to assist themselves."[3]

The charismatic perfectionists, on the other hand, lacked interest in the realities of earthly life. They did not even seek to provide protection from gyrations in the economy. Instead, otherworldly matters obsessed them. Whether Shakers, Inspirationists, or Perfectionists, they shared an outlook based either on the potential personal sanctity of the membership or on the special powers of a forceful leader. These communalists from the seventeenth century on commonly worked within the millennialist or occasionally the spiritualist tradition. Nearly all held their property in common, and they generally abhorred politics. Jacob Beilhart, the founder-leader of a late nineteenth century sect called the Spirit Fruit Society, accurately summed up the charismatic perfectionists' overall view on secular affairs. Arguing for a true religious perspective as the secret to individual happiness, he said:

> You may speak of socialism; you may speak of single tax or no tax at all; you may depend on good lawmakers and good executors to carry out those laws; you may have all material things, the necessities of life. . . . All these things will not give you peace.[4]

Radically different from the charismatic perfectionists were the new-breed pragmatists. Contemporary affairs intensely concerned them. At the heart of their credo existed the desire to test and publicize pet socioeconomic schemes. Their overriding interests centered on finding immediate and lasting relief from depression and the exploitative qualities of American capitalism. Perhaps the dark clouds of depression contained that silver lining. As an Alabama communitarian concluded in 1895, "The only way to see a rainbow is to look through the rain."[5]

While the new breeds duplicated the nonsectarianism of their cooperativist cousins, they differed on several major points. For one thing, they de-emphasized the notion of community with its homogenized lifestyles. They were merely a collection of individuals. Some, for example, might be conservative on the marriage question and conventionally moral, while others, dissatisfied with the nuclear family, favored "free love." Pragmatists, moreover, refused to retreat to the past of the independent yeoman farmer and village artisan. The technology of the day was willingly accepted; yet it had to be harnessed sensibly so as to do the greatest possible good. And these new breeds commonly expressed a keen interest in politics. There were those who even saw their colonies as vehicles to capture state governments; indeed, groups of pragmatists attempted this objective in Washington and Nevada.[6]

EVEN THOUGH the inspiration for the new-breed pragmatists to organize stemmed from hard times, the great outpouring of published works that depicted a better tomorrow acted as a powerful catalyst. Literally dozens of literary utopias espousing the pragmatist outlook appeared between 1885 and 1900, especially after the panic. The popular futuristic novels of Edward Bellamy and William Dean Howells, in particular, caused considerable initial excitement and widespread imitation during the depression. Within months after the appearance of *Looking Backward,* scores of readers decided that they could not wait until A.D. 2000. When the economic dislocations crippled the country, newly organized "Bellamy Clubs" directed an even larger stream of individuals to the burgeoning colony movement. Howells's *A Traveler from Altruria,* serialized in the *Cosmopolitan* between November 1892 and October 1893 and subsequently collected in book form, evoked a somewhat less spectacular response. Yet this "splendid dream" led directly to one significant West Coast pragmatic experiment, located near Santa Rosa, California, and appropriately named Altruria.[7]

Bellamy, Howells, and the other, albeit lesser known, futurists heartily embraced the ethic of self-help. Literary utopias were commonly created through the sacrifices of their fictional characters, ones who resembled contemporary people of good hope. These courageous and hard-working folk triumphed through sheer determination, often skirting the monopoly-dominated and corrupt political system, to create heaven on earth. The structure of daily life likewise contained various uplift devices that Americans of the day employed: community gardens, labor checks, cooperative stores, and even consumer-built railroads. Also these imaginary communitarians diligently labored through their own life cycles. Of course the wonderful technologies of the new age, based usually on electricity or perhaps some exotic power source, made living comfortable and satisfying.[8]

The writings of Charles Caryl, a Colorado businessman turned essayist, superbly exemplify this intimate relationship between self-help and literary utopia during the depression of the 1890s. The case can be made as well that the Caryl *Weltanschauung* typifies the thought of avant-garde idea people of the period.

Much of the career of Charles Willard Caryl (1858–1926) is obscure. Fortunately, his activities during the nineties are relatively well recorded. Caryl, an eighth-generation American who was born in Oakland, California, showed at an early age indications of great ambition and drive. Graduating from the Sacramento Business College at sixteen, Caryl joined the Los Angeles County government and served as the deputy assessor for two years. He then returned to Oakland and went into business for himself. In 1880 the future utopist, now twenty-one, left the West for Philadelphia. There he used his inventive skills and marketing acumen to perfect and sell a commercial fire extinguisher. Apparently this proved extremely successful financially, as John D. Rockefeller's Standard Oil Company and several other large firms purchased sizable quantities of the device.[9]

While traveling through the South during the spring of 1887, Charles Caryl became interested in that region's economic potential. Settling in Chattanooga, Tennessee, he quickly secured eastern and British capital, which he used to build several manufacturing plants. Yet trouble soon loomed. The spectacular failure of the English banking house of Baring Brothers in October 1890, which

*"One who dares to plan, for peace, happiness and prosperity for all human beings. . . ."*
Charles W. Caryl.

had invested heavily in his enterprises, caused Caryl's financial empire to collapse. Reflecting in 1897, he wrote that this setback prompted him to conclude that "the competitive struggle for wealth was wrong and must be abolished."[10]

In 1891 Charles Caryl returned to the East and launched his career as a social reformer. From then until moving to Colorado three years later he participated in the emerging social settlement movement, first in New York City, later in Boston and Chicago, and finally in Philadelphia. While his work in the former three cities is largely unknown, his labors in the latter community are documented.[11]

In February 1893 Caryl joined the staff of the new University Settlement House as resident manager. This public service agency was located in the heart of Philadelphia's worst tenement district. Initially he did a creditable job. This, coupled with his concern for the plight of the urban poor, prompted Walter Vrooman, the force behind the city's larger antislum and philanthropic organization,

"The Conference of Moral Workers," to view the ex-inventor-businessman as a dedicated servant of humanity and as a friend.[12]

Charles Caryl's good relationship with the University Settlement House and Walter Vrooman quickly soured. In April the governing board fired him, largely because of his religious activities. In his quest for a meaningful faith, which previously had led him to embrace Methodist, Presbyterian, Roman Catholic, and Theosophical doctrines, Caryl adopted Spiritualism. While at the Philadelphia center he frequently locked himself in his room where he held "conversations with departed friends" in "spiritual ecstacy." Caryl also adopted vegetarianism. His friendship with Vrooman cooled when he blasted the moral workers chief for "making of his stomach a grave yard for dead animals."[13]

The business world then saw the return of Charles Caryl. He selected Colorado as his fresh area of activity, and his new fascination was gold mining. Sometime in 1894 he arrived in Denver and acquired mineral properties along Four Mile Creek, west of Boulder, near the hamlet of Delphi. Funds came mostly from eastern financiers who seemingly subscribed liberally to stock in Caryl's Gold Extraction Mining and Supply Company.[14]

Although the energetic Caryl became a prosperous mine owner and promoter, he did not abandon his concern for the poor. Rather than involving himself in another settlement house venture, he turned to the tenets of pragmatic utopianism. In 1896 he penned a futurist work, *The New Era: A Play Introducing the Plans for a Grand New Era Model City to Be the Most Complete, Wonderful and Grand Permanent Exposition and Emporium for the Entire World*. A year later he underwrote the publication of the book in an expanded form.[15]

Caryl's *New Era* surely came as no surprise to those who knew him. Early in 1892, while working with the needy of Boston, he suggested a grandiose self-help scheme that foreshadowed his published plans for utopia. Caryl understandably sought to utilize his special capital-raising skills to achieve human uplift. Specifically, he proposed the issuance of one million shares of stock with a par value of one hundred dollars each, payable in annual installments of ten dollars. Caryl envisioned that at the end of the first year he would have ten million dollars worth of assets. With this vast sum he would acquire land along the eastern seaboard and "set 10,000 unemployed men at work building a city." The next ten million dollars would be used to buy a "forest and set more men at work getting out timber for the extension of the city." The third year

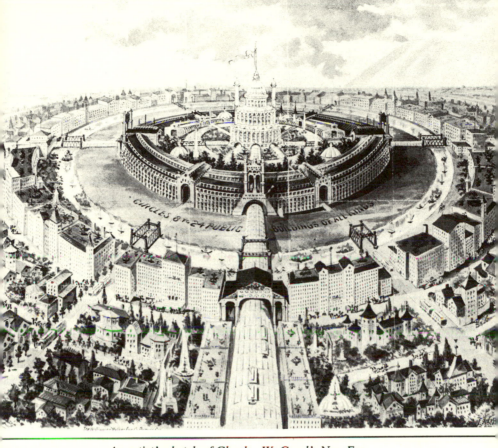

*An artist's sketch of Charles W. Caryl's New Era*
*Union Model City, published in 1896.*

would see the acquisition of coal properties and their development, while the fourth payment would underwrite a rail network between the city, forest, and mines. "Thousands more of men will be required as the work goes on. The installments as they come in will be used for the development of the manufactures of the city, the mines and the land from which the forest has been cleared." Caryl foresaw his program becoming self-supporting after the first decade and from "200,000 to 250,000 men will have been provided with homes and permanent employment." The process would continue. "Efforts will then be made to extend the scheme until eventually every unemployed man in the country will have been provided for."[16]

Few paid much attention to the Caryl plan, let alone took it seriously. Hard times had not yet settled over the face of the land. However, Edward Everett Hale, the famous author and Unitarian minister, and Robert Treat Paine, a crusading Boston philanthropist, agreed that Caryl's intentions were noble, although both logically questioned the plan's feasibility.[17]

The idea for massive self-help assistance remained in the fertile mind of Charles Caryl. The national economic calamity made his brainstorms timely; thus the appearance of the *New Era*. As he wrote in 1896, "People will now listen to me, for I can show them how to save themselves."[18]

Unlike the typical utopian treatise of the day, the Caryl work was not cast as a novel. Rather than imitating a Bellamy or a Howells, he selected a play format. The study's hero, T. A. Sutta (none other than Caryl himself), discusses his pet notions with other characters; contemporary figures (Davis H. Waite, Jane Addams, Mary Elizabeth Lease); and archtypical ones ("Mr. Railroad," "Mr. Banker," "Mr. Politician," "Mr. Oil," and "Mr. Dude"). This particular style was undoubtedly inspired by the enormously successful *Coin's Financial School,* the 1894 work of the famous silverite publicist, William H. Harvey. It was Harvey who skillfully used a series of lengthy debates on the money question to make known his inflationist concepts.[19]

T. A. Sutta (Caryl) begins with a description of the New Era Union Model City. It was to be constructed on a level tract of land, ten miles square, and would ultimately employ one million residents. Divided carefully into governmental, cultural, commercial, industrial, and residential sections, the city would be erected on a series of 239 rings around the "Administration Capitol." This magnificent structure is depicted in detail:

> The building will be three hundred feet in diameter, three hundred or more feet high, and have the highest tower or dome of any building in the world. The ground floor will be a grand central exchange depot for all the electric railways radiating to all parts of the city. The second story will be a grand Auditorium, to hold twenty-five thousand people, for important public meetings, and for the use of the Captain's Council of the New Era Union. The next floor above will be a still more beautiful grand Auditorium, though smaller, for the use of Majors' Council . . . with rooms for its officers. Above this will be the grand and magnificent Generals' Council Hall, and apartments for its officers. The floor above for the Executive Officers of the Recruits' Division and so on up, a floor for

each division of the New Era Union, to the highest or Generals' Division. Then the highest floors for the General Executive officers, and the top floor for the Supreme Council and Supreme Trustee.[20]

As Sutta suggests in his description of the Administrative Capitol, the New Era Union, like free masonry, would be divided into degrees, running from the "First or Recruit's Degree" to the "Seventh or General's Degree." The Recruits would consist of common laborers who would receive a fair wage, two dollars daily, and enjoy the eight-hour day. They would be required to purchase a Rochdale-like membership, "costing $600, to be invested in the bonds of the New Era Union, from their earnings or otherwise." Thus if a hopeful participant were penniless, he could through his own initiative help himself. The Generals would act as the executive officers and directors and would gather a daily salary of $25. They would also be asked to buy a membership of $7,500, either through investing their earnings or using their own funds. The other five degrees—Privates, Sergeants, Lieutenants, Captains, and Majors (semiskilled and skilled workers, white collar and professional people) would be paid daily salaries that ranged from $3 to $15, and they would be expected to acquire New Era Union bonds. Money raised from members would construct the Model City and pay salaries. As with Caryl's 1892 proposal, the city was to become economically self-sufficient and would sport an abundance of industries, including steel mills, railroad car–building shops, and brickworks. Bondholders would be repaid their initial investment with 6 percent interest.[21]

Sutta emphasizes that class lines, while fluid, would exist in all aspects of community life. The Generals would live in circles thirty-four through forty, the Majors in forty-one through fifty-three, and so on down to the Recruits' rings. Each class likewise would have a separate social organization, designed for its own special needs and duties. Everyone, however, would strive toward that ever-present goal of the depression period: "To attain peace, happiness and prosperity for its members, as far as possible, on a basis of justice and reciprocity."[22]

The New Era Union government rested on democratic principles. All adults, as stockholders, would annually elect a board of twelve general directors. These individuals would have charge of "all the interests of the New Era Union, subject to the supreme trustee." This person (presumably Caryl) would be elected for a ten-year term. Although this office would be a powerful one—for example, the supreme trustee would have the right to veto decisions of the general board of directors—the stockholders could initiate policy and could force referendum ballots on all legislation and decisions approved by the board and the supreme trustee. Residents, moreover, would be protected by the civil service department, which "will keep a careful account of each member's record and time of service and insure that all promotions and dismissals will be in accord with the laws of justice and reciprocity, and for the best interests of all concerned." Members also would be immune from acts of private corporate abuse, since the means of production would be cooperatively owned and managed. Similarly, all utilities were to be publicly operated.[23]

The *New Era* lays bare the Caryl world view. His primary concern centers on a way to permit the disadvantaged to help themselves. "I see my literary efforts," he told Michigan Governor-elect Hazen Pingree in December 1896, "as a way of inspiring people to dare for the best. I sometime ago saw your potato plots as the positive proof that citizens can better their condition on their own without resort to pleas to the corrupt and unhelping politicians and business leaders."[24]

Not only does the play reveal the Caryl hope for a better tomorrow realized through the existing powers of the people, but it illustrates as well his pet reform schemes—ones so commonly proposed by other pragmatic utopists: the eight-hour day, civil service, female suffrage, public ownership of utilities, and direct democracy.

Even though the *New Era* reinforced the value system of many contemporary reformers and actual utopia seekers, Charles Caryl's vision of a "meritocracy" annoyed some. Perhaps a crusty old Colorado Populist put it best: "His system of degrees of labor and wages would result in creating or containing the same old system of classes that builds up aristocracy and rotten ideas of superiority of one above another." Yet he saw Caryl as being "full of energy and good intent."[25]

During the twilight of depression Charles Caryl briefly attempted to turn his utopian dreams into reality. Using his mining properties and town lots in the Delphi mineral district as the nucleus, early in 1898 he sought to attract unemployed miners. They would receive a living wage, and profits from the diggings could then be turned over to the New Era Union development fund. By spring 1898 approximately 150 men had secured jobs in Caryl's camp—the closest the New Era Union ever came to fruition. Then in 1899 the Utopia collapsed. What interest existed flagged, due probably to the rebounding economy and the proposed class structure that likely displeased the followers. With the end to hard times the architect of the *New Era* turned his energies to business pursuits, namely coal mining and later to a bizarre eugenics scheme, "The Caryl Baby Colony."[26]

Charles W. Caryl was unusual in one respect. Virtually no fellow writers of utopian tracts during the depression era actually sought to implement their objectives. Henry Olerich, author of the futurist novel, *A Cityless and Countryless World,* commented in 1894, "I like to consider myself an original thinker who created new concepts so that we, the progressive elements, can build a better America." He later noted, "The written utopia is but a guide plan for those who desire to help themselves. I outlined what is possible today to assist the troubled among us." Indeed, Olerich did just that; *A Cityless and Countryless World,* for example, glorified public gardens, cooperative businesses, and especially the labor-check system.[27]


JUST AS A PLETHORA of utopian literary works similar to Caryl's bombarded the nation, numerous proposals for the actual creation of model societies were announced. The vast majority never progressed much beyond the good idea stage, so reminiscent of the hot-air farmers' railroad projects. Still, there was an intense desire to do something. Such suggested experiments seemingly answered the question raised by the *Twentieth Century Farmer* in 1894: "What can be done during these dark and trying days that offers anything better?" The contemporary press, reform and otherwise, repeatedly reported colony proposals. While no systematic count exists, these paper utopias totaled in the hundreds. Most appeared between 1895 and 1897, a time when proponents had collected their wits after the initial period of shock and drift.[28]

Suggestions for intentional communities graphically reveal the thrust of utopian thought during the depression. Reflecting futurist literature of the day, emphasis on the practical was universal: colonies sought to provide instant relief and to find long-range solutions to basic economic problems. Major differences came largely in matters of detail; hence these drawing-board proposals lacked a true carbon-copy flavor. Two examples suffice. One claimed Indiana origins, the other Kansas.

During the early months of 1895 newspapers contained various references to the Caryl-like dreams of a twenty-five-year-old ex-teacher from Anderson, Indiana, Truman Stewart. "A pleasing talker, a deep thinker and not lacking in energy," he seemed to possess the necessary qualifications to spark change. Rather than seeking followers from his home state, Stewart chose Boston. "He will go into the slums and will take the low and lowly. He expects to secure 5,000 people in all." Anticipating donations from public-spirited individuals to get the colony started, the young Hoosier planned to establish a self-help experiment on nearly 300,000 acres of leased Tennessee real estate within 100 miles of Memphis, and if that fizzled, his alternative was to find a comparable tract in Washington State. Once launched, this "cross between the Heavenly and Bellamy plans" would utilize a cooperative agricultural base to supply raw materials for several of the "most modern" food-processing plants. "We will enter the new century with full employment, full bellies, and full confidence that the co-operative organization is superior to the trusts."[29]

While Truman Stewart's political views are unknown, scores of Populist-backed plans for pragmatic colonies were formulated. Although apparently neither the national nor any state People's party central committees officially called for formation of such experiments, a variety of party members became directly involved. This happened in Kansas. In 1896 three prominent local Populists, state chairman and Commissioner of Banking John W. Breidenthal, United States Congressman Edwin Reed Ridgely, and former state treasurer and Kansas Alliance President William Henry Biddle, attempted to start a colony in the heart of the state's mining district, Crawford County, near the Oklahoma border.[30]

Although nothing more tangible than land options materialized, enthusiasm initially ran high. "The main idea is in caring for the thousands of unemployed that a plan of organization . . ." Breidenthal explained to the press in November 1896, "will, if put in operation, result in a few years in a prosperous, contented and happy community of home owners, employing themselves and owning their own industries, free from debt or other incumbrance. . . ." And he added, "the plan is feasible, and there is no doubt in my mind that it will be carried out successfully. The plan offers opportunities to a class who have no opportunities elsewhere."[31]

The Kansas Populists expected their Crawford County utopia to have more than primitive household industries; the proposed colony did not seek to replicate an antebellum phalanx with its small mills and workshops. "This is almost the 20th century," remarked Congressman Ridgely. "The Phalanxes of [Horace] Greeley and [Albert] Brisbane are of the musty past." These pragmatists wanted members to be engaged in production and distribution on an extensive scale, specifically operations of modern shaft mines, coal-grading and loading equipment, and rail services. "Additional large-sized operations may come in time."[32]

The Kansas Populist dream of utopia conceivably held another purpose. While the party fused successfully with the Democrats and Silver Republicans to capture the state in November 1896 and the newly elected John W. Leedy administration seemed to offer solid, honest government, John Breidenthal, for one, felt that an intentional community might be a means of helping to sustain Populism. "A stable expanding community will constantly remind people of the purpose of the People's [party] mission," he told an Iowa friend in January 1897. "It could well become a living monument to the best our people can do." Simply, the Crawford County utopia would be to Populism what the Maple and Freedom communes were designed to do for the Labor Exchange.[33]

NOT ALL PRAGMATIC UTOPIAN HOPES went unfulfilled. Colonies materialized. Some disappeared quickly, usually falling prey to the common banes of intentional communities: inadequate capital, internal tension (often disagreements over authority and long-term objectives), and beckoning economic opportunities elsewhere. Others proved more durable. Ruskin Co-operative Association (Tennessee), Altruria (California), Equality (Washington), Co-operative Brotherhood (Washington), Fairhope Industrial Association (Alabama), and the Christian Commonwealth (Georgia) testify to experiments that measured their histories in years and not months.[34]

As colony names themselves suggest, specific ideologies varied. Once more Americans sought no single pathway to a better world. For example, the Brotherhood of the Co-operative Commonwealth emphasized the tenets of democratic socialism. This group expected to make their Equality, Washington, community the working model for utopia; in fact, this Debs-inspired band attempted to capture the state for its advanced brand of liberalism. The nation's single-taxers, on the other hand, found uplift based on the doctrines of Henry George to be more attractive than Debsian socialism. Their famous experiment, launched in 1894 at Fairhope, Alabama, became the practical laboratory for this widely discussed economic scheme. And liberal Christians, swayed by the Social Gospel, saw the messages of the New Testament as practical guides for helping the poor. The "Golden Rule" of "Comrade Jesus" that all people should be good friends and that society should be one big, harmonious neighborhood seemed especially appropriate for the times. While the Christian Commonwealth near Columbus, Georgia, best exemplifies a pragmatic Christian-inspired intentional community, similar colonies appeared. For instance, the Christian Co-operative Association, located near Clay Center, Kansas, sought to "afford help for the needy who will *help themselves,* protection for the weak, and those who join it, if they stay by it, especially of the younger folk, may enjoy a Christian community."[35]

While variations exist, these new-breed pragmatic colonies showed a keen interest in politics. Unquestionably the vast majority of members lacked the designation of apolitical. The popular thought embraced populism or, as that crusade faltered, socialism. An intentional community might see itself as the core unit in an attempt to dominate an entire state or region or merely to serve as a liberal force in a local setting. As the *Altrurian,* a leading utopian organ of the mid-1890s, put it, "The excitement in colony building is expected to bring about much . . . [including] the practical means of expanding the powers of the people through political centers that will surely keep the fires of reform burning with a red-hot intensity."[36]

As with "paper" colonies, hard times explain the formation of the tangible utopias. Julius A. Wayland, father of the Ruskin experiment, said it best in late 1896: "With depression we are seeing the actual creation of the ideal communities throughout the length and breadth of the land because the times make such places essential." Added Wayland, "Through our own good sense and hard work we can turn hopelessness into real promise. . . . We do not have to wait for Bryanites or the Pops to do it for us," although admittedly he was willing to help.[37]

Two themes dominate the relationship between the depression and intentional communities. Some individuals flocked to these experiments largely to escape the ravages of desperate times. "I selected the Fairhope Industrial Colony on Mobile Bay," recalled a member of this well-known single-tax colony, "because I lost my job in the [coal] mines of Mahaska Co. [Iowa] in 1894 and I had no money and couldn't easily stay there for long but I wanted to help myself and the family." He surprisingly admitted, "I had never read George although I knew he offered the larger hope for [the] country's economic and social evils, so I joined these people from Oskaloosa and Des Moines." Yet individuals chose life in an intentional community for highly altruistic reasons. Reminiscing in 1945, Ralph Albertson, cofounder of the Christian Commonwealth, typified a common sentiment: "The purpose common to us all was to demonstrate the practicability of the law of love in industrial life. And by this we meant literally what we said."[38]

As with most potato patch and labor exchange proponents, a sizable number of communitarians, perhaps a majority, viewed their activities as ephemeral: "temporary havens of relief for those willing to help themselves during the hard times." Some thought that colonies should "come and go," that is, come during depression and go during prosperity. "All we would need to do would be to engage people to keep these places in readiness." Presumably colony facilities, too, would be "mothballed."[39]

Resembling some other self-help advocates, there were those utopists (and here undoubtedly a significant concentration) who perceived their particular uplift scheme as a vehicle for *permanent* change. "Colonies are the ways to a honest and better world, the only ways. If the country is to be redeemed, it is not likely to come from the big parties, but from the pops and this colony idea." They logically distinguished between the merely temporary settlement and the one designed to endure. "I heartily approve of the Salvation Army putting surplus labor on waste land," expounded an Altruria backer, "but they are seeking but a partial solution to the question of the unemployed." America, according to this viewpoint, required more than just the expansion of the "poor-farm" concept.[40]

At times the dual objectives of relief and reform caused severe distress. Without doubt, this is a leading explanation for the demise of this brand of utopia. When the poor and middle-class mingled (one contemporary observer categorized them as "riff-raff" and "good people"), differences of opinion regularly developed over a colony's purpose. Drifters seeking a temporary shelter and idealists expecting to reform the world understandably failed to share the same long-term aspirations or to express equal enthusiasm for community living. Nasty fights therefore erupted over what one com-

*A rare view of Long Lane, Missouri, shows the store (left) of the Home Employment Co-operative Company, ca. 1897.*

munitarian called a "seemingly irresolvable situation when people have different goals and where one group could wreck the other with ease." Specifically, members who wanted only a passing refuge usually lacked money to contribute to the utopian cause, and by the time their labors made a significant contribution, they abandoned community life to the hard-core visionaries for better positions elsewhere.[41]

A closehand view of two colonies, the Home Employment Co-operative Company and the Colorado Co-operative Company, indicates the nature of self-help found in the pragmatic utopian experiments. Even though these settlements shared common characteristics, particularly when it came to their association with the depression, they were hardly duplicates of one another.

The Home Employment Co-operative Company was the brainchild of William H. Bennett (1833–?). While material on Bennett's career is often tantalizingly hard to find, it is known that this New York state native expressed interest in communitarianism as early as 1871. In August of that year, Bennett, then a struggling merchant in the Mississippi River town of Red Wing, Minnesota, announced: "I shall start in about four or five weeks to Southern Kansas to obtain a location and commence a Community." It is not clear the type of colony he had in mind, although Fourier "association" thought probably appealed to him.[42]

Like the typical proponent of utopia, William Bennett expressed optimism about his future endeavor. Noting that he had "two pair of mares, one stallion, one mare colt of two years, two new wagons and my store goods," he admitted that he would not be able "to raise much cash" and that "people say I am foolish and can't make it work." But affirmed Bennett: "I say I will and believe I can."[43]

The budding utopist never reached his original destination in frontier Kansas. He selected Missouri instead. Alcander Longley, the state's nonpareil communitarian and quintessential cooperativist, influenced this decision. A veteran of various utopian episodes since his teens, Longley had recently abandoned his first Missouri colony, Reunion, a tiny commune based on Fourier-Brisbane principles near the Ozark town of Carthage. Eager to found still another "perfect" experiment, he met Bennett in northwest Missouri through a common friend and asked him to join his proposed "Friendship Community" in Dallas County, in the state's southwestern section. Bennett agreed. On December 29, 1871, William and Emily Bennett and their son Edward arrived in Buffalo, the Dallas County seat, to begin their communal efforts.[44]

In its early days the Friendship Community seemed promising. Even though the cooperativist colony attracted only a handful of members, it operated a general store and hotel in Buffalo and acquired five-hundred acres of good quality land west of the town. Construction of a large communty house on the farm was soon under way. Then a split occurred. Bennett, his family, and a few other members withdrew in a personality dispute with Longley. Although Friendship soon crumbled, and Longley and his faithful band left the area, the Bennett group remained. About 1875 he launched his own Friendship-like colony, Enterprise, near the Dallas County hamlet of Long Lane. Apparently the national depression that followed the Panic of 1873 produced some local interest in a cooperative community experiment. In February 1877 Bennett, for unknown reasons, liquidated most of his real-estate holdings. He then disappears from the historical record until the mid-1890s.[45]

During the darkest days of the nineties depression, William H. Bennett concocted still another utopian scheme. This time he largely abandoned the notions of Fourier and Longley and embraced the tenets of the new utopian pragmatism. "Our system," he wrote in 1895, "is a good deal on the plan of the Ruskin [Tennessee] Commonwealth," although like most "modern" contemporary experiments the basic economic structure paralleled the older cooperative format. All the means of production were owned by the membership and used for its benefit. Supporters bought or earned company stock with profits divided in proportion to an individual's investment. Yet major differences existed. Bennett himself noted that "[members] can conduct their personal life as they see fit." Unlike Friendship or Enterprise the goal was definitely not to seek an ordered milieu. And differing from the older secular schemes of the 1870s, Bennett sought to enjoy and to popularize several reform concepts common to the Populist-Progressive era. The offices of president, secretary, treasurer, and the five trustees would be elected biennially, with every adult having an equal vote. The popular veto of the initiative and referendum would likewise insure democracy. Male members would work the sought-after eight-hour day, while females were to toil two fewer hours. "All work is paid for by the hour and in scrip or checks, redeemable in necessary articles of maintenance, and may be redeemed in cash at the convenience of the company."[46]

William Bennett called his Missouri experiment the Home Employment Co-operative Company (HECC), a name reflective of its mission. Why he bothered to attempt utopia building again and to alter dramatically the format are open to speculation. Bennett's fear of the country's drift toward industrial monopolies, "where the trust dominates all," and the coming of hard times, where "businesses ruin all, even those who sweat daily or want to, by their speculative and senseless antics," probably propelled him to seek a workable alternative to the status quo. But his longing for that "cooperative world where all are free of exploitation and all benefit fully from there [sic] labor" did not mean rejection of current technology and creation of the type of society envisioned by antebellum and Gilded Age cooperativists like an Alcander Longley. Bennett willingly accepted the industrial age. To his way of thinking "electricity especially means big benefits for the all . . . and big bus[iness] can . . . mean benefits for the all." Like fellow newbreed utopists, he viewed large-scale corporations useful only "if they are willing to place the interests of the commonwealth ahead of their own, which they presently do not."[47]

The Bennett *Weltanschauung* took on tangible dimensions

when the HECC embarked upon a modest program of mutual endeavor. While endorsing the concept of large-scale cooperative manufacturing, Bennett's colony, resembling typical contemporary pragmatist ventures, relied on cottage-type industries for its economic livelihood. Soon the HECC colonists operated a "broom factory, a [flour] mill, a barber shop and a blacksmith shop." A shingle mill and a small cannery were also launched. Colony land produced the necessary raw materials: broom corn, wheat, fruits and vegetables, and some lumber. Business activities remained primitive because there were never more than forty members at any one time. As Bennett said tartly, "You can't expect a steel mill."[48]

Although theoretically the HECC accepted the calling of advancing reform—namely to popularize the concept of the democratic cooperative commonwealth—it seemingly attracted an unsupportive following. Colonists consisted mostly of individuals down on their luck who merely wanted a place to weather the economic storm. Specifically, the majority of the initial participants consisted of former miners from the tri-state mineral belt and ex-railroaders from the nearby towns of Springfield and Lebanon. Even though the membership throughout its history held a liberal persuasion—records from the colony precinct (Long Lane, Wilson Township) show that it provided the only overwhelmingly Populist vote in the county in 1896 and again in 1898—the overall complexion of the HECC residents apparently changed dramatically from its formative days in 1894–1895 to its final years early in the twentieth century. In one of his few extant letters, the HECC founder-leader observed shortly before the colony's collapse, "I held the opinion that those early joiners wanted to change the country, but I was wrong. I quickly came to learn that their commitment to an altered way of living for all was as fleeting as a summer rainbow when their former positions were once more available." And he lamented, "I found myself operating a work farm, not a breeding place for those who would bring about important change." By the time the HECC folded the dozen or so members were probably those either dedicated to Bennett's grand scheme or unable to make a living elsewhere. Without doubt the HECC served as a place for immediate self-help rather than as a living laboratory for the advancement of economic and political reform.[49]

Regardless of members' intentions and expectations, William Bennett and his fellow colonists wholeheartedly accepted the work ethic. Bennett made it clear from the experiment's inception that the HECC "will welcome those who are ready to roll up their

*The Colorado Co-operative Company developed*
*the Tabeguache Park area of western Colorado*
*after 1894. "The soil . . . is deep and rich."*

sleeves and work, there are no berths for kid-glove gentry, or those
who want to live off other people's labors." This dedication to
what he called "solid business" caused neighbors to accept readily
the members. The HECC escaped the hostility that intentional colonies, especially religious ones, experienced because of unorthodox
practices. Recalled one resident: "That Bennett group worked
hard. There was no nonsense in Long Lane. No funny types with
funny sex interests or funny living habits or crazy church notions.
They were just mostly people out of work who tried hard to get
back on their feet." Said another, "No chippies [prostitutes] or
dudes there. . . ."[50]

Officially organized in Denver on February 11, 1894, the Colorado Co-operative Company (CCC) consisted of a more diverse lot
than the HECC. Its membership roll contained mutual colonizers
who had lost money and nearly their lives in the ill-fated Topolo-

bampo, Mexico, colony of the Kansas-Siñaloa Investment Company; unemployed miners from Front Range diggings; railroad and streetcar employees (who had either been blacklisted for their union activities or were simply out of work); a few Colorado artisans and poverty-stricken farmers; and a band of financially solvent but deeply altruistic advocates of cooperative socialism.[51]

As a body, the CCC sought the typical aims of a pragmatic secular utopia. Its supporters desired immediate relief from the ravages of depression and the demonstration of the workability of "Capitalistic Cooperation." Writing in the maiden issue of the *Altrurian,* the colony newspaper, President P. A. Simmons argued, "We do not look for any relief on political lines for years to come. I, therefore, maintain that through cooperative methods only will any *immediate* relief come to the masses." With great optimism he later described the period:

> The sunlight of cooperation is breaking through the dark clouds of competition—the dreams of "Looking Backward" is being realized in a practical way; and if through adversity the people have been brought to study the principles of cooperation with a view to bettering their condition, the suffering caused by the panics of the past year or two, will not have been in vain.

Like fellow idealists, Simmons believed that cooperation would be the wave of the dawning century—that a cross section of Americans would abandon competition for this more humane and predictable way of life.[52]

When speaking of "Capitalistic Cooperation" the CCC referred to its specific organization. The company prospectus, paralleling a Rochdale store and the Caryl and Stewart proposals and closely resembling the HECC, called for an issue of $100,000 of capital stock divided into one thousand shares at a par value of $100 each. These would then be sold for cash or for labor or products of practical use to the endeavor. Money generated from the sale of stock would be used "to own and operate manufactories . . . [and] to build homes for its members." The company would employ only stockholders, each of whom would receive twenty cents an hour, payable at first in stock or food supplies from the central store and eventually in cash. Individual ownership of property would be allowed, even encouraged, although the maximum amount of land was to be limited to forty acres. As in the William Bennett experiment, the means of production (mills, shops, and the like) would be cooperatively run. Utilities were to be publicly owned and operated. Politically, all CCC members would participate equally. Actions of the democratically elected president and board of directors were subject to possible vetoes by the rank and file through the initiative and referendum process. (This reform tool—direct democracy—was one that colonists wanted the larger society to adopt.)[53]

Work would ensure success. Members realized that cash was in short supply but "muscle is to be found everywhere." The philosophy of self-help permeated the experiment. *"We are here to help ourselves and our fellow brethren,"* proclaimed President Simmons. "If you can but will not work, you are not to share in the economic benefits of the Company which will surely come. The lazy had better know where the Co. stands on this matter for we are not going to tolerate hammock sleepers." No one publicly challenged this position. "Either you work or you starve," remarked one member. "I will always be happy to do the first." He added, "That is why I came. . . ."[54]

Just as the CCC supporters accepted the time-honored tenets of toil, they matched other contemporary self-help proponents. Reminiscent of the labor exchange, work could be traded for company stock; frankly, that was the only practical method for the distribution of securities. Duplicating community gardeners who sought free or inexpensive land, the Colorado utopists eyed vacant government real estate. "Capitalistic Cooperation" was not to be realized in Denver, but rather on an arid mesa in the Tabeguache Park region of Montrose County, on Colorado's west slope.[55]

In 1895 ten men and one woman arrived in the wasteland from Denver. While worthless without water, the site selected held bright promise.

> The soil . . . is deep and rich. It is protected on all sides by mountains and is free from destructive winds and cyclones. There are vast coal deposits near by and abundance of timber for lumber and fuel. Fine building stone and beds of fire clay in vast quantities are close at hand—in fact nearly everything for the building up of a strong and independent community, can be had for the taking.[56]

By depression's end the ranks of the hearty pioneers increased to nearly 130 and a variety of cottage industries (printery, harness shop, and sawmill) flourished at Nucla, the main settlement. Significant work had been accomplished by company "ditch gangs" on what ultimately would be a 17-mile-long arterial canal that claimed the nation's tallest and longest irrigation flume, the 108-foot-high and 840-foot-long cottonwood trestle.[57]

Life was no picnic. Tasks were hard and members endured a mostly bean diet. Still the routine had its pleasant side. The company, for one thing, sponsored an assortment of social functions, most of which were held in Association Hall.

> The members, old and young, volunteer recitations, readings, music, original essays, poems, ethical talks, etc., and the evening passes so pleasantly that all regret its flight. A dance is held in the same place nearly every Saturday evening and a dramatic club produces plays and dialogues.

As might be expected, political discussions proved exceedingly popular.[58]

Unlike the old breed cooperativists, these Colorado pragmatists sought political action. While the membership never tried to capture the Centennial state, individually they nearly always backed reform-oriented candidates, Populists during the 1890s and Socialists after the turn of the century. While politically of a similar mind, the CCC, unlike traditional utopias, lacked a strong sense of community cohesion. "Each person was expected to tend to his own business and people just did not try to ride herd over others. . . . 'Free-love' wasn't supported, but most could tolerate it."[59]

The CCC not only experienced the predictable internal squabbles mostly triggered by personality conflicts, but it also encountered the seemingly universal split between individuals who joined for solely economic reasons and those who expressed a more idealistic bent. One no-nonsense colonist, E. L. Gallatin, attacked two "dreamers," members L. L. Miller and L. L. Gifford, in his sparkling autobiography, *What Life Has Taught Me,* as ones "who were full of theoretical socialism, and could lean on a shovel handle and build castles for a king." They soon left.[60]

The departure of visionaries like Miller and Gifford, who as idlers might be readily expelled, did not mean that "advanced thinkers" were absent. Although there is no evidence that a Luddite mentality existed among the membership (everybody, for example, endorsed the latest irrigation technology), a serious and prolonged quarrel developed over the company's future direction. While the experiment's economic base was largely agricultural, some stockholders stressed the desirability of expanding manufacturing and the overall urban dimensions of the colony. They

*The modest main street of Nucla (Piñon) sported that recently built look in 1899 (above). It looked more substantial about 10 years later (below), the time when the Colorado Co-operative Company voted to disband as a purely co-operative experiment.*

dreamed of Nucla becoming more than a frontier settlement. These members sought to make it a model city of 10,000 to 15,000 residents, where "gardens, parks, schools, lyceums, theaters, art galleries, music halls are to be built and enjoyed by all." Their community was to be both a "city beautiful" and a "city useful." The best urban planners would be hired to design attractive yet functional commercial, residential, and manufacturing districts. High-speed, publicly owned electric trolley lines would connect the irrigated lands with the central metropolitan core so that "no farm people will be forced to live in isolated areas where they have little chance of enjoying the companionship of others."[61]

A variety of cooperatively owned manufacturing firms would be launched. "We need farm machinery, canning, packing and other large plants," argued one colonist. "This will be one way that the PEOPLE can break the back of the great trusts. Our population can be both the producer and the consumer." Unemployment would be unlikely since "we are all part of the Company" and "demand for Company products will likely be strong in the New West and elsewhere." These idealists enthusiastically but understandably endorsed the work ethic: "There shall be no room for the idler, the adventurer or speculator." Nucla, moreover, would become the example for what these members hoped would be other pragmatic communities. "We will show Americans how they can sensibly solve the great economic and political problems that we always seem to face. Why there is plenty of tillable land in Colorado alone to support extensive co-operative city colonies." The fundamental roadblock to the achievement of this grand objective was the "inability of the [CCC] membership to work long and hard for the better way." Namely, the vast majority contentedly accepted the company's limited agricultural focus.[62]

In an unusual twist, the "Soldiers of Cooperation"—the idealists—drifted away from the CCC before those who sought only relief from hard times. Some of the latter stayed for decades, even though the company disbanded in 1909 as a purely cooperative venture. The reason was the "ditch." In the spring of 1904 water at last flowed to its final destination; the individually owned parcels suddenly mushroomed in value. Hundreds of acres of sagebrush and prickly pear cactus quickly gave way to orchards, vegetable patches, and grain fields. Colonist Eugene Hopkins recalled:

> I believed in the cooperative way, but at Tabeguache Park those who were willing to help themselves stayed to turn a desert into valuable property. Those diehards, and they were some of the most intelligent people I ever knew, failed to change the world to cooperation, so they left in disgust because of what they saw as selfishness of the laboring majority who desired *only* their water rights and plots of ground to become valuable so they would never have to worry and suffer hard times again.

*The CCC's most spectacular construction effort was its 17-mile irrigation canal that sported this 108-foot-high and 840-foot-long cottonwood trestle.*

Even though the cooperative spirit flagged, the CCC succeeded at perhaps its most important goal: "It builds homes for the homeless."[63]

AMERICAN UTOPIAN THOUGHT during the depression of the 1890s contained important elements of the self-help credo. Futurists, as a whole, were serious, practical individuals who deeply hoped society could be dramatically improved without reliance on the political process. Although much effort went into printed works and "paper" colonies, concrete experiments also emerged.

Intentional communities offered the more adventurous and determined souls outlets to improve their own lot and perhaps change the course of history. From the chronicles of established colonies, demonstrated by experience at the CCC, the "hangers-on" found little comfort among the rank and file. The triumph of utopists who held only the narrow world view of life—to get back on their feet financially—is perhaps understandable. Either they left the colony to the "advanced thinkers" as occurred at the HECC, or as in the case of the CCC, they stayed but abandoned the grander principles of "Cooperative Capitalism." Not to be forgotten, however, was the duality of purpose found in other self-help schemes—the desire for "instant relief" and the hope for a permanent alteration of American life. Of course not all pragmatists agreed on what the precise formula should be.

> I came away from Nucla knowing that only the motivated people will likely try to help themselves, but for what purpose. To put bread on their family table or on the tables of all mankind? I never could figure out how much effort had to be expended to make the big changes. I guess it really can't be achieved unless human nature is altered for the better.[64]

# Self-Help Brought Up to Date

ROSPERITY failed to return with any degree of permanence with the dawning of the new century. Downward slippages have occurred rather regularly from 1900 to the present. During the past three decades, for example, the economy has faltered badly in 1948–1949, 1957–1958, 1973–1975, and again today. Major disaster, however, struck in 1929 when the bull market crashed, an event that precipitated the Great Depression. Almost every American felt some discomfort during the 1930s, but millions of industrial workers, particularly the unskilled, and small and tenant farmers experienced enormous hardships.

While the New Deal gave relief and World War II restored prosperity, the country witnessed then and during other periods of economic tightness and national emergency a resurrection of self-help concepts. In recent years, though, the socioeconomic environment has changed noticeably from the nineties. Several bursts of monumental reform activities produced safety-net programs—social security, unemployment insurance, Medicare, and the like—that most Americans have come to accept as the government's proper obligation to its citizens. Still, individuals during the thirties, especially, remembered the responses of the 1890s. Noted a writer for the *Detroit Free Press* in 1933:

> I recall vividly my neighborhood surviving on vegetables from those plots we had back in the '90's. Again I see much interest in gardening by Detroiters. Individual and public gardens can solve much of the personal suffering of the unemployed here and elsewhere.[1]

Indeed, the old potato patch scheme pioneered by Detroit Mayor Pingree represents superbly the continued popularity of self-help devices. The "Liberty Gardens" and "Victory Gardens" of the era of the two world wars reveal instances when Americans in large numbers turned to vegetable growing. Literally tens of thousands of food-producing parcels replaced weed patches, rubbish heaps, and even manicured lawns nationwide. But the country's reliance on gardens is better seen in the "antiinflation" plots that blossomed forth in the 1970s. Unmistakably the reason for the massive current-day revival of potato patches is more closely related to those forces that gave rise to them initially—hard times and not war.

"Antiinflation" gardens grew rapidly after the national economy took a nosedive in 1973. Not only did the newly formed National Association for Gardening emerge to coordinate an estimated thirty thousand organized community gardens by 1974, but millions more individually either discovered or rediscovered the value of a backyard plot. As in the 1890s, gardens of the seventies were not so much adult recreation as they were easily obtainable and effective weapons in the war on the skyrocketing cost of living. Remarked Mark Cassidy, Director of the Los Angeles, California, Neighborhood Gardens and Farms program in 1975: "the high cost of food, unemployment and insecurity about the future seem to be among the main factors that have motivated people to grow their food. By gardening it is possible for a family to save several hundred dollars a year on food." Cassidy might have given an identical explanation for the concept's widespread popularity eighty years earlier. Interest in gardening is tied to the economy; in fact, potato patches might be viewed as a crude economic indicator. In relatively prosperous 1971, for example, about 29 percent of American households produced vegetable crops, but soaring prices boosted that percentage to 47 percent in 1974 and to 49 percent a year later. A stronger economy caused the percentage to slip badly in 1976 and 1977. Then as food prices climbed dramatically in 1979 and 1980 along with double-digit unemployment and inflation so did self-help food production, increasing to near the levels of 1974–1975.[2]

Perhaps the best example of the renewed popularity of self-help gardens is found in Detroit, Michigan, the home of those pioneer Pingree Potato Patches. In 1975 the city's compassionate and energetic mayor, Coleman A. Young, initiated the "Farm-A-Lot Program." This modern-day Pingree plan is just as simple. Farm-A-Lot personnel ask citizens merely to find a suitable vacant publically owned lot (Detroit has thousands), and then visit one of the dozen "Neighborhood City Halls" for a free gardening permit and seed kit. Those who wish to plant on their own land can likewise receive complimentary seeds. Soon after its establishment the Farm-A-Lot Program offered assistance for larger growing projects, ones designed for block clubs, school organizations, church groups, or several families. Not only has the experiment saved thousands of participants hundreds of dollars annually but it has provided additional benefits, albeit ones long associated with such activities. Noted William Buford, who gardened in an empty city lot near his Tennessee Street home in 1980, "I just like growing stuff. Besides, when you're gardening you can't get any closer to nature unless you're in the ground."[3]

A twist to the Pingree plan that has gained popularity of late is the so-called gleaner movement. It is in the tradition of the ancient Hebrew practice of farmers leaving a portion of their harvest ungathered for the poor, the activity that Jean-François Millet so vividly caught on canvas in 1857. Elderly, low-income Americans, especially those who live in vegetable-rich areas like central California and south Florida, have sought to help themselves and others by becoming full-time scroungers. They glean produce that otherwise would go to waste—either plowed under in the field or left to rot at the packinghouse. As agriculture and food processing become more highly mechanized and farm labor more costly, vast amounts of edible fruits and vegetables go unpicked or unpacked. Growers and processors usually allow the needy to have access to this food, saving them the trouble and expense of having the raw produce removed.[4]

In 1975 several score of older residents of Sacramento, California, led by a retired stockbroker, launched an all-volunteer group they called Senior Gleaners. Within a few years this bootstrap organization had become the largest of similar efforts nationally; by 1979 its 1600 members acquired some 6000 tons of produce that they distributed among themselves and other deserving souls. The rules are simple: a person must be fifty or older and willing to work in some capacity. Healthy, able-bodied members pack, sort, and distribute, while the less able conduct office tasks. Senior Gleaners ask supporters to contribute two dollars monthly (if they feel they can afford it) to pay for operating their six donated trucks and the utilities at the headquarters building, a former school near downtown Sacramento. A vice-president, Peggy Rand, explained the movement's purpose:

> The need for self-help programs especially among the low income elderly has long been evident. Many small gleaning

groups have developed as a result not only of the economic needs, but as a sort of "breaking out" from the four-wall cages that surround them in their inactive home lives.

And she noted that "the phenomenal expansion of Senior Gleaners is a direct result of our being able to offer them an opportunity to help themselves."[5]

Downswings in the economy since the turn of the century have repeatedly caused the appearance of labor exchange–like schemes. And like the earlier locals they are usually small, urban based, and temporary. Recently barter clubs have become common. Usually these self-help voluntary groups, perhaps organized by a consumers' league or a community action council, provide swap deals on a vast array of goods that range from used cars for home furnishings to children's toys for lawnmowers. Some issue "checks" for services. A plumber might cash his scrip with a mortician or electrician. Similarly, some metropolitan dailies have given readers space to run brief advertisements that offer exchange deals. The weak economy of late also has led to the creation of the Oklahoma City–based Barter Systems. Since 1976 this firm has arranged various corporate trades for a minimal charge. For example, it helped a rubber company exchange a jet airplane for $1.3 million of coal, and it assisted a California bank in obtaining print advertising for $1.9 million worth of boats that it acquired when a client went bankrupt.[6]

While G. B. De Bernardi and his supporters probably would have approved such activities, they more likely would have been intrigued or even enthusiastic about the monetary notions of the self-taught economist, Ralph Borsodi (1886–1977), father and chief proponent of a novel money scheme. The Borsodi plan initially appeared during the immediate post–World War II years, when its author devised a medium of exchange that could fight the evils of inflation. This modern-day De Bernardi developed a currency based on "indexation," namely notes that enjoyed redemption in fixed amounts of thirty basic commodities (gold, silver, oil, wheat, wool, and the like). Thus theoretically an inflation-proof or "constant" currency resulted. Essentially, the Borsodi money was nothing more than shares in a pooled investment, but unlike stocks and bonds that need to be cashed in order to be spent, constants circulated as money.[7]

For years there was only limited interest in Ralph Borsodi's alternative currency. But as the fierce inflation spawned by the Arab oil embargo of 1973 began to empty the pocketbooks of Americans, Borsodi discovered growing fascination with his pet project. The blueprint was revived when several hundred residents of his hometown, Exeter, New Hampshire, embraced the concept. Moreover, the plan caught the attention of the media.[8]

Although in his mideighties, Borsodi personally organized the experiment. He told his Exeter backers to pool their available financial resources, buy commodities, and then write checks—"constant certificates"—on their investments. Individuals exchanged dollars for constants; a friendly bank coordinated the plan. Just as labor exchange scrip once circulated among merchants, Exeter participants spent their new money for everything from corn chowder and wheat bread at the Load and Ladle to hairdos at Beau Reve Beauty Salon. Partakers' purchasing power stayed in step with increases in the dollar price of local goods and services. Although termed successful as an antiinflationary tool, the Exeter episode ended in late 1974 after more than a year when the Securities and Exchange Commission opposed it. This federal watchdog agency disliked the similarity between constant certificates and unlisted, unregulated securities. When liquidation occurred, a person who paid $20.00 for 100 constants at the beginning of the program got $23.30 when the accounts closed—a return well above the then rate of inflation.[9]

The persistence of the cooperative spirit, more so than labor exchange–like devices, indicates splendidly the linkage between self-help actions of the 1890s and twentieth century efforts of private uplift. During the past eighty years literally thousands of cooperative enterprises have appeared throughout the length and breadth of the land. Some have been short lived, usually springing up during a time of economic adversity and then melting away when prosperity returns. A cooperative store in Beaver, Boone County, Iowa, illustrates this genre. Created in 1929, this concern functioned for nearly a decade until better times caused its dissolution. Its organizational structure resembled earlier mutual ventures as well as contemporary and latter-day ones. The store bought mercantile goods—groceries, hard and softwares—for townspeople and farmers alike at discount prices and subsequently passed the savings on to its consumer-members. (A token fifty cent annual fee allowed anyone to join.) Of course overhead costs existed—rent, utilities, shipping, and the salary of a manager-secretary—but they were modest. While an ephemeral self-help venture, the Beaver business served a valuable purpose. As one member put it: "This place is just the thing for the hard-up folks in the neighborhood to assist themselves . . . and to make ends meet." He added, "Barter can go only so far," referring to the widespread practice, especially during hard times, of the exchange of goods and services rather than money. "There are items you can't trade for, so that's why the store is necessary."[10]

Not all twentieth century examples of the cooperative business have been temporary or for that matter operated on a small scale. The Farmers' Educational and Cooperative Union of America, better known as the Farmers' Union, the direct descendent of the Alliance movement, has systematically launched and sustained cooperative enterprises since the dawn of the century. Its farm supply cooperatives have for years blanketed the Upper Plains, and its Grain Terminal Association is one of the world's largest grain marketing agencies. In much the same vein, Farmland Industries (formerly Consumers Cooperative Association), which dates from 1929, has grown to an enormous size. By the late seventies this Kansas City–based cooperative boasted annual sales in excess of $3 billion and claimed some 500,000 farmer-members in 2,300 local units. While both organizations have experienced failure, the development of proven business practices, especially of late, has made them successful. Not so long ago these agribusiness cooperatives were still dominated by founders who could sign up members with evangelical zeal but who lacked professional management skills. But this has ended. During recent decades the Farmers' Union, Farmland Industries, and other big coops have turned regularly to promising college graduates and to the executive suites of their corporate competitors for their managers.[11]

The giant agribusiness cooperatives have gained considerable cooperative company. At least five thousand debuted during the 1970s. While their range of products and services is extensive— everything from eye wear to legal counseling—the vast majority deal with foodstuffs, and many are operated as not-for-profit concerns. Unlike the Farmers' Union and Farmland Industries cooperatives, the more numerous consumer businesses are likely to be financially fragile and modest in size. Indeed, these leaders of the new wave of coops, untouched by the profit motive, tend to be stronger on goodwill than on business expertise—much like the officials of cooperative stores historically.[12]

While not a carbon copy of the Beaver, Iowa, enterprise of the

1930s, the Food Advisory Service (FAS) of the San Francisco Bay area, started in the mid-1970s, is another part of the continuing grass-roots self-help cooperative movement. The specific purpose of this nonprofit venture is simple: to sell to older persons groceries at a price lower than commercial retailers do. The several score of FAS volunteers dedicated themselves "to seeing that the elderly stretch their precious food dollars for the best quality and quantity," and "to give an opportunity for the disadvantaged to help themselves." Food is bought in bulk, packaged, and delivered by vans to minimarkets, housed in churches, recreation centers, and apartment buildings. And just as the labor exchange launched enterprises to employ the poor, the FAS subsequently started a satellite organization, Gallery Faire Enterprises. Operated physically within FAS's food warehouse, the business is a profit-making packaging and assembly concern. Elderly workers receive both wages and food coupons to box such merchandise as audio headsets for airlines, gift items, and pharmaceuticals and stationery supplies.[13]

While the farmers' railroad concept died by the twentieth century, the notion of consumer-owned carriers remained very much alive. The idea has been expressed repeatedly and with greater frequency during the past decade. There is every likelihood that it will continue to be a dimension of the story of intercity freight transportation.

Examples abound. One early illustration is the saga of the tiny Illinois Midland Railroad Company. Built in 1913 to link two Kendall County communities, Millington, located on the Chicago, Burlington and Quincy's Aurora-Streater branch, with rail-starved Newark, three miles to the southeast, the Midland typified shortlines of the era. It was constructed and operated by outside capitalists for maximum profits. But when the line encountered severe financial difficulties during the immediate post–World War I recession, owners of a Newark elevator leased it for a twenty-year period. After area farmers organized the Newark Farmers' Grain Cooperative Company in 1935, their new business acquired the private elevator and its rights to the Midland. Several years later when the lease expired, the cooperative bought the railroad and ran it until the 1950s when the trucking of grain became more convenient. The self-help philosophy of this farmer rail operation is succinctly contained in this statement made by the road's general manager at the time of the property's purchase: "We had to enter the railroad business because the Q [the Chicago, Burlington and Quincy] wouldn't serve our Newark elevator. We needed a rail outlet. Either we help ourselves or go bust.''[14]

Recently the theme of self-help has become much more evident. The merger madness that infected railroading during the 1960s and the faltering industry in the seventies meant that thousands of miles of trackage became unwanted. Seemingly countless consumers faced the reality of no more trains. Midwestern farmers experienced more line abandonments than any other business group, for granger roads merged with regularity (the Chicago and North Western for example, absorbed two rivals that served the nation's breadbasket, the Minneapolis and St. Louis in 1960 and the Chicago Great Western eight years later), and most roads suffered from extremely poor financial health. One patient, the once-mighty Chicago, Rock Island and Pacific with more than seven thousand route miles, died in the spring of 1980. Another one-time giant, the Chicago, Milwaukee, St. Paul and Pacific, at the same time decided to contract radically in order to survive.

To protect themselves financially, agrarians have repeatedly entered the railroad business. Desperate farmers are attempting currently to devour portions of the Rock Island's carcass (also rolling stock, depots, and the like). AGRI Industries, a major Iowa cooperative, is seeking to obtain bits of the Rock, about 900 miles, in order to save a transportation service that is considerably cheaper than trucks for long-distance grain hauling. The recently formed Atlantic and Pacific Railway Corporation, likewise farmer affiliated, is hoping to control 750 miles of former Chicago, Rock Island and Pacific trackage, including the mainline from Council Bluffs, Iowa, to Chicago. (This is the exact territory that the American Railway Company sought to serve back in the 1890s.)[15]

While optimism is expressed about the future of "farmers' railroads," recent history contains tales of failures equal to those that almost universally characterized the self-help rail efforts of the nineties. One episode that is reminiscent of Farmer Hines's ill-fated Duluth and North Dakota pike is the defunct Great Plains Railway. In 1973 more than five hundred farmers who lived along a recently abandoned eighty-mile Chicago and North Western branch in the corn and sorghum country of southeastern Nebraska decided to keep their rail outlet. As one of the seventeen on-line elevator managers said, "Farmers know they'll get 10–15¢/bu more for their grain . . . since elevators won't have to discount for higher truck shipping costs." So the Great Plains Railway was born. Even though the Chicago and North Western gladly sold the property and the infant company enjoyed widespread local support, the farmer-operators immediately encountered serious difficulties. The roadbed had deteriorated badly. Rehabilitation proved impossible, even though the new owners bought thousands of cheap but good used ties and other salvaged materials. For two years the GRIN (the road's official initials) struggled to be the "Greatest Railroad in Nebraska," but poor track conditions resulted in the last run on April 15, 1975. *Successful Farming*'s prediction that "If it's true that 'the good Lord helps those that help themselves,' this group of Nebraska farmers is on the way to salvation" proved to be wrong. Fortunately, the loss to the farmer-investors was minimal compared to other business failures. The GRIN's scrap value proved to be considerable. Unfortunately, the demise of this road meant that transportation bills skyrocketed.[16]

A final example of the resurgence of the self-help phenomenon in the recent past is related to the renewed popularity of the utopian or "intentional" community. Thousands have appeared since the beginning of the now largely spent counterculture or "hippie" movements of the 1960s and early 1970s. Most of these small and short-lived colonies have attracted individuals who had become disenchanted with life in America's postindustrial society. "I want freedom from cops, straights, and fat-cat capitalism" seemed a common expression of motivation. While many opted for religious experiments, best characterized by Stephen Gaskin's highly successful charismatic perfectionist "Farm" in Tennessee and fanatic Jim Jones's ill-fated People's Temple of California and later Guyana, others selected secular settlements. Whether residents of Drop City in Colorado or Morning Star Ranch in California, these communitarians typically embraced psychedelic drugs, Eastern mysticism, and back-to-the-land notions. Admittedly, the vast majority of individuals who have joined the current wave of colony making differ dramatically from those who participated in utopianism during the depression of the 1890s. Yet some have sought a haven from economic troubles; others, too, have enlisted to offer solutions to national problems.[17]

The self-help theme is unmistakably part of the utopian Catholic Worker Movement. Started in New York City in 1933 to feed and clothe the poor, most of whom had lost jobs due to the Great Depression, this small band of altruistic Roman Catholics led by Dorothy Day (1897–1980) by the midthirties expanded its operation from merely being an urban mission on a tough, gritty street near the Bowery to include several work farms. The most important one was located near Tivoli in New York's Hudson River valley; this settlement became a place where the poor could become self-reliant and where all could benefit from the labors of the many. By World War II the organization had spawned more than a score of rural farms, usually connected with "hospitality houses" in various metropolitan centers. While its pacifist thrust and good times caused the Catholic Worker Movement to decline during the war period and the subsequent era of prosperity, a combination of lean years, antiwar sentiments, and rampant materialism has given the tiny organizational core renewed life recently. The Tivoli Farm, which in the late 1970s claimed about fifty inhabitants, is still designed "to provide a home away from the city for the poor and needy regardless of religion, race or creed." And the colony "makes it possible for the down-and-out to help themselves": members farm, publish a sometimes monthly newspaper, *The Catholic Worker,* make craft objects, and host retreats and conferences for their general maintenance. Donations constitute an important source of annual income. As a community of need, the group does not seek actively to change society. (Founder Dorothy Day looked to the person rather than to mass action to transform society. Indeed, she repeatedly admitted that she had little in common with reform and never sought the overthrow of capitalism and its network of property relationships.) Some supporters, however, subscribe to the tenets of anarchism: "the abolition of the state and its replacement by a federation of communities."[18]

While the Tivoli settlement resembles the Salvation Army communities of the 1890s, the Padanaram Colony might be viewed as a modern-day Colorado Co-operative Company. Located in a heavily timbered section of southern Indiana, this cooperative venture is a community of "free-thinkers" who have opted for a communal life-style based on a mutually owned wood-cutting business. Most of the seventy-five inhabitants joined Padanaram because area jobs were scarce and living precarious. Daniel Wright, the founder of the enterprise, explained the settlement's organization in the late sixties "as the clear thing to do. People couldn't support themselves here, so I gave them a way to upgrade their lives through their own labors." But unlike the Piñon, Colorado, experiment of the mid-1890s, Padanaram members do not see their Indiana community as a harbinger of the new age. While some residents believe that as the national economy falters their model might be more widely emulated, they have not created the utopia militant. "We have no desire to contact the outside world," said one participant in 1975. "We are totally content to help ourselves."[19]

The idea that a utopian colony is willing to remain apart from the mainstream of American life represents the sentiment of the vast segment of contemporary communards. Some do see their experiments as having a possible impact on the larger society. Those who toy with "low-tech" devices—wind, solar, and animal power, for instance—who use organic food and fiber, and who make a commitment to ensuring rigid environmental standards, often believe their efforts to be on the cutting edges of an advanced and appreciably better life-style. "Our place might very well encourage the thoughtful that they can assist themselves and the big society if they think about what we are presently doing here," wrote one Arizona nature commune member in 1979. "People have more control of their destiny than they could ever possibly think." And there are a few political action communes, although their numbers have diminished markedly since the end of the Viet Nam conflict. Members of these utopias are committed, practicing activists who are dedicated to the purpose of changing the social system.[20]

THE THRUST of self-help efforts in recent America is largely devoid of the concept of fundamental reform. Certainly toilers in the self-help crusades of the 1890s also generally sought immediate relief from problems associated with hard times, but, as demonstrated in the five studies, a discernible element of uplift characterized each.

There is only limited indication that current-day participants in the community garden, barter, farmer-owned railroad, or even intentional colony projects regard their efforts as anything more than either short- or long-term self-help. The story of present gardening ventures reveals this superbly. Linked to the 1890s crusade were "radical" single-taxers, individuals who fervently felt that publicly owned vegetable plots might be an important step toward implementation of their beloved pet reform. For the most part, the single-tax craze died with the Great War and the waning of the Progressive spirit. Gardens today are for food and not food for thought. Barter clubs also are designed to meet prevailing economic needs rather than a challenge to established business practices. Yet the hard-core disciples of the late Ralph Borsodi view constant currency as a suitable permanent change in monetary matters in much the same way as G. B. De Bernardi and his staunch supporters envisioned the future of the labor exchange. Borsodi shortly before his death argued that his self-help plan contained the element of eventual financial salvation: "The economic well-being of nations in the free world would be assured and the debacle into which inflation is now leading them would be prevented." Farmer-railroads, while expected to become permanent transportation institutions, are not considered as likely replacements for private carriers nor as enterprises that might lead to nationalization of the rail net. "We are picking up the pieces of an industry that is in terrible shape. . . . We are keeping stems and branches alive for the public good." No messianic fervor is found among this self-help body. At first glance, it might be assumed that all proponents of intentional communities look toward their labors as models for the larger society to emulate, whether those dedicated to a particular set of religious ideals or those imbued with some notions of the desirability of the "low-tech" society. Although the latter are occasionally in the tradition of late nineteenth century communitarians, the once widespread gusto for revolutionizing the populace is mostly gone. "They just withdraw . . . do their own thing and enjoy for themselves what they know is the good life."[21]

More exceptions exist with the cooperative impulse. Leaders of the ever-growing farmer mutuals commonly see their firms as ultimately dominating the agribusiness sector. Recent complaints to Congress about the federal government's preferential policies toward these consumer-owned enterprises by such private agribusiness giants as W. R. Grace, Monsanto, and Ciba-Geigy graphically indicate the validity of their competitors' boastful predictions. In an era of aroused consumers—the Nader phenomenon of the 1960s and 1970s—cooperative ventures in general are understandably seen by increasing numbers of citizens as *the* viable alternative to the incumbent brand of capitalism. "The spectacular success of various co-ops," contends one proponent:

> is going to mean a drastic change in the future complexion of the business community. I predict that more and more people will want to apply democratic principles to business and to do something positive about the unreasonably high prices that are being extracted from the general public for sky-high profits and wasted corporate expenditures.[22]

Logically, the question arises as to why the reform element has been less evident in contemporary self-help efforts, at least when compared to the 1890s. The plausible explanation is that this initial response to the ravages of an industrial depression occurred in an environment that offered scant protections by government. As "Potato Patch" Pingree observed, "Until such time as society has learned to do justice to all, we must depend on the methods nearest at hand." Many questioned the role of the church, school, and government and embraced the notions of the Social Gospel, reform social Darwinism, and public-interest consumer politics to make these institutions relevant for the times. This continued agitation for society's improvement led to a myriad of reform victories during the Progressive era and eventually to the programs of the New Deal, Fair Deal, and Great Society. The creation of the American version of the welfare state offered protections that were dreams at best for those who experienced the greatest episode of hard times.[23]

Whether or not designed to alter American life, self-help efforts are an amazingly valuable part of modern history. They demonstrate how individuals today and in the future might find relief and regain their self-confidence during times of economic stress. Yet they are more than merely examples of a usable past. Improvement efforts conspicuously show the ingenious American mind at work. Responses to difficult situations have led to diverse commonsense approaches. While not always successful, they have succeeded with some frequency. The actuality of "what is past is prologue" is limited; still, the self-help saga reveals nicely that people should not panic when adversity strikes. Americans are tough; it is still true that often the down-and-out can pull themselves up by their bootstraps. There truly exists a way to combat powerlessness, that nameless dread.

# *Notes*

PREFACE

1. David P. Thelen, *The New Citizenship: Origins of Progressivism in Wisconsin, 1885-1900* (Columbia: University of Missouri Press, 1972), p. 2.
2. W. Allen Black to Hazen S. Pingree, Nov. 1, 1896, Hazen S. Pingree Papers, Burton Historical Collection, Detroit Public Library, Detroit, Mich. (hereafter cited as BHC); *Mirror* (St. Louis), May 1, 1897.
3. *Rocky Mountain News* (Denver), June 6, 1895; Hazen S. Pingree, "The Future of America," (n.d.), Hazen S. Pingree Papers, BHC.

INTRODUCTION

1. *Commercial and Financial Chronicle* (New York), Sept. 16, 1893.
2. See Lawrence Goodwyn, *Democratic Promise: The Populist Moment in America* (New York: Oxford University Press, 1976), pp. 25-31; William E. Laird and James R. Rinehart, "Post-Civil War South and the Great Depression: A Suggested Parallel," *Mid-America* 48:206-10 (July 1966); Alex M. Arnett, *The Populist Movement in Georgia* (New York: Columbia University Press, 1922), pp. 49-75; C. Van Woodward, *Origins of the New South* (Baton Rouge: Louisiana State University Press, 1951), pp. 175-88.
3. Gilbert C. Fite, *The Farmers' Frontier, 1865-1900* (New York: Holt, Rinehart & Winston, 1966), pp. 34-74, 94-136; O. Gene Clanton, *Kansas Populism: Ideas and Men* (Lawrence: University Press of Kansas, 1969), pp. 18-20; Fred A. Shannon, *The Farmer's Last Frontier: Agriculture, 1860-1897* (New York: Holt, Rinehart & Winston, 1945), pp. 291-95.
4. John D. Hicks, *The Populist Revolt: A History of the Farmers' Alliance and the People's Party* (Minneapolis: University of Minnesota Press, 1931), pp. 54-95; U.S., Department of the Interior, *Eleventh Census of the United States: 1890; Report on Farms and Home* (Washington, D.C.: Government Printing Office, 1897), pp. xiii, 1-16, 55-134; Allan G. Bogue, *Money at Interest: The Farm Mortgage on the Middle Border* (Ithaca: Cornell University Press, 1955), pp. 2-4, 268-72; *Iowa State Register* (Des Moines), June 15, 1895; *Omaha Bee,* Feb. 7, 1891.
5. *Alliance Herald* (Stafford, Kans.), May 29, 1890.
6. *Statistical Abstract of the United States, 1908* (Washington, D.C.: Government Printing Office, 1909), p. 248; Doane Robinson, *Doane Robinson's Encyclopedia of South Dakota* (Private publication, 1925), pp. 603-5; *Dakota Ruralist* (Huron, S.D.), Aug. 9, 1891.
7. Williard L. Thorp, *Business Annals* (New York: National Bureau of Economic Research, 1926), pp. 29-81; Phyllis Deane, *Abstract of British Historical Statistics* (Cambridge: Cambridge University Press, 1962), pp. 472-73; Arthur F. Burns and Wesley C. Mitchell, *Measuring Business Cycles* (New York: National Bureau of Economic Research, 1946), pp. 78-79; Frank P. Weberg, *The Background of the Panic of 1893* (Washington, D.C.: Catholic University of America Press, 1929), pp. 3-8.

8. Charles Hoffman, *The Depression of the Nineties: An Economic History* (Westport, Conn.: Greenwood, 1970), pp. 50–54; Albert H. Imlah, "British Balance of Payments and Export of Capital, 1816–1913," *Economic History Review* 5:208–39 (1952).

9. *Railway Age and Northwestern Railroader,* Feb. 24, 1893; *New York Times,* Feb. 21, 1893; *Wall Street Journal,* Mar. 1, 1893; *The Nation* 56:175 (Mar. 9, 1893); Albert C. Stevens, "Analysis of the Phenomena of the Panic in the United States in 1893," *Quarterly Journal of Economics* 8:124–48 (Jan. 1894); *New York Herald,* Apr. 24, 1893; W. Jett Lauck, *The Cause of the Panic of 1893* (Boston: Houghton Mifflin, 1907), pp. 118–19; George Rutledge Gibson, "The Financial Excitement and Its Causes," *The Forum* 15:483 (June 1893).

10. *New York Times,* May 4, 1893.

11. Gerald Taylor White, "The United States and the Problem of Recovery after 1893" (Ph.D. diss., University of California, 1938), pp. 1–3; Arthur Stone Dewing, *A History of the National Cordage Company* (Cambridge, Mass.: Harvard University Press, 1913); *Mankato* (Minn.) *Review,* Apr. 12, 1892; *Cordage Trade Journal,* Feb. 15, 1893.

12. *New York Times,* May 8, May 11, 1893; *New York Herald,* May 27, 1893; *Chicago Tribune,* May 8, May 9, May 11, 1893.

13. Hoffman, *Depression of the Nineties,* pp. 63–89; Clarence D. Long, *Building Cycles and the Theory of Investment* (Princeton: Princeton University Press, 1940), p. 216; Samuel Rezneck, "Unemployment, Unrest and Relief in the United States during the Depression of 1893–97," *Journal of Political Economy* 61:324–45 (Aug. 1953).

14. U.S., Department of the Treasury, *Annual Report of the Secretary of the Treasury, 1893* (Washington, D.C.: Government Printing Office, 1894), p. 351; Victor Selden Clark, *History of Manufactures in the United States* (New York: Peter Smith, 1949), 2:99, 101, 303; *Poor's Manual of Steam Railroads* (New York: Poor's, 1900), pp. lxxi–lxxii; Walter W. Price, *We Have Recovered Before! A Comparison of the Present Depression with the Major Depressions of the Past Century, 1837–1857–1873–1893* (New York: Harper and Brothers, 1933), pp. 79–80. The magnitude of hard times is reflected in the dramatic drop in the use of smoking and chewing tobacco. Internal revenue from these products fell off in three months, July through September 1893, by more than 50 percent.

15. Carlos C. Closson, "The Unemployed in American Cities," *Quarterly Journal of Economics* 8:168–217, 257–60 (Jan., Apr. 1894); Albert Shaw, "Relief for the Unemployed in American Cities," *Review of Reviews* 9:29–37, 179–91 (Jan., Feb. 1894).

16. *Southern Mercury* (Dallas), Jan. 17, 1894; J. W. Bennett, "The Cause of Financial Panics," *Arena* 7:493 (Mar. 1894); "The Relief of the Unemployed in the United States during the Winter of 1893–94," *Journal of Social Science,* pp. 1–51 (Nov. 1894); Charles D. Kellogg, "The Situation in New York City during the Winter of 1893–94," in *Proceedings of the National Conference of Charities and Corrections,* ed. Isabel C. Barrows (Boston: National Conference of Charities and Corrections 1894), pp. 21–30; *Iowa State Register,* Jan. 10, 1895; *Ottumwa* (Iowa) *Daily Courier,* Mar. 2, 1895.

17. *Iowa State Register,* June 9, 1895.

18. Ibid., Jan. 13, 1895.

19. Uriel H. Crocker, *The Cause of Hard Times* (Boston: Little, Brown, 1893), p. 10; *Herald* (San Antonio, Fla.), Dec. 3, 1893.

20. Charles H. Bullard to Ethel Petri, Sept. 20, 1893, Charles H. Bullard Papers, Minnesota Historical Society, St. Paul (hereafter cited as MHS); *Cleveland Citizen,* Aug. 5, 1893; *Twentieth Century Farmer* 1:12 (Apr. 1894).

21. David P. Thelen, *The New Citizenship: Origins of Progressivism in Wisconsin, 1885-1900* (Columbia: University of Missouri Press, 1972), pp. 57-85; H. Roger Grant, *Insurance Reform: Consumer Action in the Progressive Era* (Ames: Iowa State University Press, 1979), pp. 17-19; *Parnell* (Mo.) *Sentinel,* Aug. 24, 1895.

22. Allan Nevins, *Grover Cleveland: A Study in Courage* (New York: Dodd, Mead, 1933), pp. 523-24; *The Nation* 52:147-50 (Feb. 19, 1891).

23. James D. Richardson, *A Compilation of the Messages and Papers of the Presidents* (New York: Bureau of National Literature, 1917), 13:5828; *New York Post,* July 1, 1893; *New York Tribune,* July 2, 1893.

24. Alexander D. Noyes, "The Financial Record of the Second Cleveland Administration," *Political Science Quarterly* 12:189-211, 561-88 (June, Dec. 1897); *Denver News,* Aug. 29, 1893; *Omaha World-Herald,* Aug. 29, 1893.

25. For a copy of the Omaha Platform see George Brown Tindell, ed., *A Populist Reader* (New York: Harper and Row, 1966), pp. 90-96.

26. *The Advocate* (Topeka, Kans.), Apr. 25, 1894; U.S., Congress, House, *Congressional Record,* 53d Cong., 3d sess., Feb. 5, 1895, pp. 1795-97.

27. William McKinley, *The Tariff in the Days of Henry Clay and Since* (New York: Henry Clay Publishing, 1896); F. W. Taussig, "The Tariff Act of 1894," *Political Science Quarterly* 9:585-609 (Dec. 1894); F. W. Taussig, *The Tariff History of the United States* (New York: G. P. Putnam's Sons, 1931), pp. 327-52; *Nation* 64:256 (Apr. 8, 1897); Samuel T. McSeveney, *The Politics of Depression: Political Behavior in the Northeast, 1893-1896* (New York: Oxford University Press, 1972), pp. 32-62.

28. W. T. Stead, " 'Coxeyism': A Character Sketch," *Review of Reviews* 10:52 (July 1894); *The Champion* (New Whatcom, Wash.), May 5, 1894; "The Coxey Non-Interest Bond Bill," Jacob S. Coxey Papers, Ohio Historical Society, Columbus (hereafter cited as OHS).

29. Thorstein Veblen, "The Army of the Commonweal," *Journal of Political Economy* 2:456-57 (June 1894); William D. P. Bliss, *Encyclopedia of Social Reform,* s.v. Peffer, William A.; Donald L. McMurry, *Coxey's Army: A Study of the Industrial Army Movement of 1894* (Boston: Little, Brown, 1929), pp. 127-292.

30. *Ottumwa Daily Courier,* Aug. 12, 1895; *Champion,* May 5, 1894; *Progressive Thinker* (Chicago), June 2, 1894; *Iowa Referendum* (Newton), Apr. 1894; *Progressive Thought and Dawn of Equity* (Olathe, Kans.), June 1894.

31. Ignatius Donnelly to Charles Canning, Jan. 2, 1894, Ignatius Donnelly Papers, MHS; *Nation* 57:482 (Dec. 28, 1893); *Fort Dodge* (Iowa) *Messenger,* Jan. 10, 1895; *Progressive Thought and Dawn of Equity,* Aug. 1894.

32. Hicks, *The Populist Revolt,* pp. 292-93; "Governor Waite's Proposal," *Review of Reviews* 9:197-98 (Feb. 1894).

33. William Fillmore to Ignatius Donnelly, Nov. 29, 1893, Ignatius Donnelly Papers, MHS; Frances G. Peabody, "Colonization as a Remedy for City Poverty," *Forum* 17:52-61 (Mar. 1894); *Cleveland Citizen,* Sept. 16, 1893; Samuel M. Jones to W. H. Morehouse, Jan. 8, 1898, Samuel M. Jones Papers, OHS.

34. W. S. Green to Hazen S. Pingree, July 29, 1896, Hazen S. Pingree Papers, Burton Historical Collection, Detroit Public Library (hereafter cited as BHC); *Knoxville* (Tenn.) *Sentinel,* Feb. 18, 1896; *Southern Mercury,* Dec. 6, 1894; *Chicago Herald,* Mar. 5, 1894.

35. Josephine Shaw Lowell, "Methods of Relief for the Unemployed," *Forum* 16:653-62 (Feb. 1894); Leah Hannah Feder, *Unemployment Relief in Periods of Depression: A Study of Measures Adopted in Certain American Cities, 1857 through 1922* (New York: Russell Sage Foundation, 1936), pp. 72-73; S. H. Cummings to Samuel M. Jones, n.d., Samuel M. Jones Papers, OHS; *Twentieth Century*

*Farmer* 1:10 (Apr. 1894); "The Co-Operative Farm," *Review of Reviews* 13:349 (Mar. 1896).

36. E. R. L. Gould, "How Baltimore Helped the Idle," *Forum* 17:497-504 (June 1894); *Baltimore Sun,* Jan. 15, Feb. 2, 1894; *Sound Money* (Massillon, Ohio), Jan. 26, 1895.

37. *Weekly Gazette* (Steubenville, Ohio), Apr. 20, 1894; Feb. 1, Feb. 15, 1895; Aug. 1, 1898.

38. *Ottumwa Daily Courier,* Aug. 13, 1895.

39. Nathaniel Shurtleff, ed., *Records of the Governor and Company of the Massachusetts Bay in New England* (Boston: William White, 1853), 1:405; "The Perversion of Charity," Nov. 19, 1893, Washington Gladden Papers, OHS.

40. Freeman Champney, *Art & Glory: The Story of Elbert Hubbard* (New York: Crown, 1968), p. 91.

41. See James B. Gilbert, *Work without Salvation: America's Intellectuals and the Discovery of Alienation, 1880-1910* (Baltimore: Johns Hopkins University Press, 1977); Daniel T. Rodgers, *The Work Ethic in Industrial America, 1850-1920* (Chicago: University of Chicago Press, 1978).

42. Washington Gladden, "Relief Work," *Review of Reviews* 9:38-39 (Jan. 1894); *Progressive Thought and Dawn of Equity,* July 1895.

43. Lowell, "Methods of Relief for the Unemployed," pp. 655-62; "Relief for the Unemployed," *Review of Reviews* 9:319 (Mar. 1894).

44. Arthur W. Milbury, "The Industrial Christian Alliance of New York," *Review of Reviews* 11:55-59 (Jan. 1895); *Detroit Tribune,* Dec. 4, 1895.

45. James D. Richardson, *A Compilation of the Messages and Papers of the President, 1789-1907* (Washington, D.C.: Bureau of National Literature and Art, 1908), 3:344; *New York Herald,* Nov. 6, 1873; Samuel M. Jones to Henry D. Lloyd, May 28, 1897, Samuel M. Jones Papers, OHS.


CHAPTER ONE

1. Frederic W. Speirs, Samuel McCune Lindsay, and Franklin B. Kirkbridge, "Vacant-Lot Cultivation," *Charities Review* 3(Apr. 1898).

2. Melvin G. Holli, *Reform in Detroit: Hazen S. Pingree and Urban Politics* (New York: Oxford University Press, 1969), pp. 62-64; *Detroit Evening News,* Dec. 2, 1893; U.S., Department of Agriculture, Division of Statistics, *Report of the Experience of Detroit* (Washington, D.C.: Government Printing Office, 1895), p. 7; *New York World,* May 12, 1895.

3. Holli, *Reform in Detroit,* pp. 3-4; *Dictionary of American Biography,* s.v. "Pingree, Hazen S."; Charles R. Starring, "Hazen S. Pingree: Another Forgotten Eagle," *Michigan History* 32:132 (June 1948); William Stocking, "New England Men in Michigan History," *Michigan History Magazine* 5:130 (Jan.-Apr. 1921).

4. Holli, *Reform in Detroit,* pp. 6-8; Fred C. Hamil, "Charles H. Smith, Junior Partner of Pingree and Smith," *Michigan History* 45:45 (Mar. 1961). While Pingree's later life contained numerous triumphs, the sudden death of his nineteen-year-old daughter, Gertrude, on March 26, 1893, was an enormous personal tragedy. See *Michigan History Magazine* 11:465 (July 1927).

5. Holli, *Reform in Detroit,* pp. 23-124; William P. Belden, "Governor Pingree and His Reforms," *American Law Review* 34:36-50 (Jan.-Feb. 1900). Although a Republican, Pingree became much admired by the political left. For example, the *Southern Mercury,* a leading voice of the Farmers' Alliance, concluded in its issue of Nov. 26, 1896, that the Detroit mayor "is not far from being a good populist."

6. Cyril and Marjorie Player, "Hazen S. Pingree: The Biography of an American Common Place," unpublished manuscript, 1931, Burton Historical Collection, Detroit Public Library (hereafter cited as BHC); *Detroit Sunday News-Tribune,* June 10, 1894; Hazen S. Pingree, *Facts and Opinions; or, Dangers That Beset Us* (Detroit: F. B. Dickerson Company, 1895), p. 159. Captain Gardener himself remarked that "it was about the 10th of June last year [certainly before June 6, 1894] that it occurred to Mr. PPingree, while driving along the Boulevard in Detroit, that could but the poor and unemployed get a chance to cultivate some of the vacant and idle lands there. . . ." Ibid., p. 161.

7. *Detroit News,* June 6, 1894; "To the Ministers and Pastors of Detroit," Hazen S. Pingree Papers, BHC; *Detroit Journal,* June 7, June 11, 1894; George B. Catlin, *The Story of Detroit* (Detroit: Detroit News, 1926), pp. 615–16.

8. *Detroit News,* June 13, June 15, June 16, 1894. Mayor Pingree's sale of "Josie Wilkes" cost him dearly. Valued at $1,315, the horse brought a mere $387. Fortunately, the circus raised about $500. See "To Be Sold at Auction," broadside in Hazen S. Pingree Papers, BHC; Player, "Hazen S. Pingree," p. 207; *Detroit News,* Jan. 26. 1901.

9. *Report of Agricultural Committee, Detroit, Mich.: The Cultivation of Idle Land by the Poor and Unemployed* (Detroit: n.p. 1894), pp. 3–5; Memorandum signed by A. C. O'Connor (ca. 1894) in Hazen S. Pingree Papers, BHC; Player, "Hazen S.Pingree," p. 208; *Detroit Tribune,* June 19, 1894.

10. *Report of Agricultural Committee,* 1894, p. 5; Pingree, *Facts and Opinions,* pp. 164–65; *Detroit Tribune,* Sept. 22, 1894.

11. *Detroit Evening News,* Aug. 15, 1894; *Report of Agricultural Committee,* 1894, p. 5.

12. Ibid., pp. 6, 8; Pingree, *Facts and Opinions,* p. 165; B. O. Flower, "A Successful Experiment for the Maintenance of Self-Respecting Manhood," *Arena* 15: 545–54 (Mar. 1896).

13. *Detroit Free Press,* June 7, 1894; James T. Eaman to Hazen S. Pingree, June 6, 1894; Hazen S. Pingree Papers, BHC; *Detroit Free Press,* June 7, 1894.

14. *Report of Agricultural Committee,* 1895, pp. 3, 5.

15. Ibid., p. 3.

16. *Report of Agricultural Committee,* 1898, p. 3; ibid., 1901, p. 5. During the twilight years the "lots for the most part were planted by old people, widows, deserted wives, etc., who regardless of the times are more or less dependent on charity." *Report of Agricultural Committee,* 1899, p. 3.

17. *Report of the Agricultural Committee,* 1896, p. 9.

18. *Chicago Tribune,* Apr. 1, 1895; *New York World,* May 12, 1895; *Minneapolis Tribune,* Sept. 1, 1895; *Denver Times,* June 4, 1895; *Buffalo News,* Oct. 15, 1895; *Steubenville* (Ohio) *Weekly Gazette,* May 3, 1895; *Winona* (Minn.) *Republican,* May 2, 1895; Bolton Hall to Hazen S. Pingree, May 15, 1896; Hazen S. Pingree Papers, BHC; *Once-A-Week* (New York), June 30, 1894; David F. Moreland to Hazen S. Pingree, Oct. 19, 1894, Hazen S. Pingree Papers, BHC. Some communities were slow to consider the Detroit Plan. The editor of the *Iowa State Register* (Des Moines) of Apr. 3, 1895 wrote that "It is strange that this form of self-help did not commence sooner. How is it in Des Moines and other Iowa cities? . . . These times are bringing people to a realization of necessity, the healthfulness and the nobility of gardening."

19. *New York World,* May 12, 1895; *Cleveland Citizen,* Nov. 17, 1894.

20. W. Morris Deisher to Hazen S. Pingree, Jan. 23, 1897, Hazen S. Pingree Papers, BHC; Board of Supervisors, Erie County, New York to Hazen S. Pingree, June 25, 1894, BHC; *Buffalo Express,* Nov. 13, 1895; *Vacant-Lot Cultivation* (New York: Association for Improving the Condition of the Poor, 1898), pp. 5–12; *The*

*A.I.C.P. Annual Report, 1895* (New York: Association for Improving the Condition of the Poor, 1895), pp. 2-4.

21. *Vacant-Lot Cultivation,* pp. 8-9; Charles A. Brown to Hazen S. Pingree, Mar. 6, 1896, Hazen S. Pingree Papers, BHC.

22. *New York World,* Mar. 16, 1895; Apr. 21, 1895; *New York Mail and Express,* Mar. 18, 1895; *New York Tribune,* Apr. 12, 1895; *Voice* (New York), Mar. 28, 1895; *New York Press,* June 30, 1895.

23. *New York World,* Oct. 27, 1895; *The A.I.C.P. Annual Report, 1895; Indianapolis Sentinel,* Feb. 3, 1896; "Vacant City Lot Farms," *Review of Reviews* 13:349 (Mar. 1896); Michael A. Mikkelsen, "Cultivation of Vacant City Lots," *Forum* 21:313-17 (May 1896).

24. *New York World,* Mar. 16, 1895.

25. *Norfolk* (Va.) *Bulletin,* Nov. 23, 1895; Seattle *Intelligencer,* May 4, 1895; *St. Joseph* (Mo.) *Herald,* Apr. 3, 1895.

26. E. R. Moses to Hazen S. Pingree, Apr. 30, 1896, Hazen S. Pingree Papers, BHC.

27. W. D. Cornell to Hazen S. Pingree, Mar. 23, 1896, Hazen S. Pingree Papers, BHC.

28. See Henry George, *Progress and Poverty: An Inquiry into the Cause of Industrial Depressions and of Increase of Want with Increase of Wealth* (New York: J. W. Lovell, 1879).

29. Paul and Blanche Alyea, *Fairhope, 1894-1954: The Story of a Single Tax Colony* (University, Ala.: University of Alabama Press, 1956); H. Holmes to Hazen S. Pingree, Oct. 15, 1895, Hazen S. Pingree Papers, BHC.

30. *Wilmington* (Del.) *News,* Feb. 28, 1896; *Justice* (Wilmington, Del.), Dec. 1, 1896.

31. Arthur Power Dudden, *Joseph Fels and the Single-Tax Movement* (Philadelphia: Temple University Press, 1971), pp. 35-39; Joseph Fels to Hazen S. Pingree, Dec. 30, 1896, Hazen S. Pingree Papers, BHC.

32. Quoted in Dudden, *Joseph Fels,* p. 39.

33. Gould to Hazen S. Pingree, Nov. 26, 1895, Hazen S. Pingree Papers, BHC.

34. *Missouri Valley* (Iowa) *Eye,* Mar. 11, 1895; *Dakota Ruralist* (Huron, S.D.), Oct. 4, 1894.

35. *News* (Savannah, Ga.), Apr. 5, 1895; *Report of Agricultural Committee,* 1896, p. 9.

36. *Chicago Tribune,* Apr. 7, 1895.

37. *Iowa State Register,* Apr. 2, 1896; *Washington Post,* Apr. 27, 1895.

38. *Buffalo Express,* Nov. 12, 1895; S. A. Pierce to Hazen S. Pingree, Mar. 16, 1897, Hazen S. Pingree Papers, BHC.

39. *Brockton* (Mass.) *Times,* Oct. 9, 1895; *Saturday Review* (Des Moines), Oct. 19, 1895; *Philadelphia Press,* Mar. 7, 1897.

40. B. O. Flower to Hazen S. Pingree, Nov. 20, 1896; Hazen S. Pingree Papers, BHC; *Los Angeles Times,* Mar. 28, 1896; Samuel A. Murray to Hazen S. Pingree, Aug. 17, 1896, Hazen S. Pingree Papers, BHC.


CHAPTER TWO


1. *The Labor Exchange; What We Are* (Independence, Mo.: Labor Exchange Publications, 1894), p. 6.

2. *G. B. De Bernardi: A Sketch and an Appreciation of His Life* (n.p., n.d.); *Independence* (Mo.) *Sentinel,* May 17, 1901.

3. *Progressive Thought and Dawn of Equity* (Olathe, Kans.), Dec. 1897.

4. Ibid.; *G. B. De Bernardi.*

5. Marshall, Mo.: Capital Parlor Print, 1890.

6. Ibid., esp. pp. 9-11; *Progressive Thought and Dawn of Equity,* Dec. 1894.

7. G. B. De Bernardi, *Synopsis of the Labor Exchange* (Independence, Mo.: Labor Exchange Publications, n.d.); *Progressive Thought and Dawn of Equity,* Sept. 1894, Oct. 1894.

8. Ibid., Oct. 1894.

9. E. Z. Ernst, *The Progressive Hand Book of the Labor Exchange* (Olathe, Kans.: Labor Exchange Publications, 1895), pp. 30-32.

10. Ibid., *Free Press* (Devils Lake, N.Dak.), Feb. 20, 1896; F. W. Cotton, "The Labor Exchange," *Arena* 14:141-43 (Sept. 1895); *Thirteenth Annual Report of the Kansas Bureau of Labor and Industrial Statistics, 1897* (Topeka: State Printer, 1898), pp. 204-7; *Coxey's Sound Money* (Massillon, Ohio), May 22, 1897.

11. *Progressive Thought and Dawn of Equity,* Jan. 1895.

12. Ibid., Sept. 1893; Oct. 1893; Mark Holloway, *Heavens on Earth: Utopian Communities in America, 1680-1880* (New York: Dover Publications, 1966), pp. 119-21; Ray Reynolds, *Cat's Paw Utopia* (private publication, 1972), pp. 24-36.

13. Edward Bellamy, *Looking Backward, 2000-1887* (Boston: Ticknor, 1888), see especially Chapter 9.

14. *Progressive Thought and Dawn of Equity,* June 1894.

15. *Cleveland Citizen,* Aug. 24, 1895; Eugene Higgins to Hazen S. Pingree, Apr. 1, 1895, Hazen S. Pingree Papers, Burton Historical Collection, Detroit Public Library.

16. *Bakersfield* (Calif.) *Populist,* June 6, 1895; *Progressive Thought and Dawn of Equity,* Nov. 1897; *What Is the Future?* (Independence, Mo.: Labor Exchange Publications, 1897), p. 1.

17. *Progressive Thought and Dawn of Equity,* Sept. 1896; May 1898.

18. R. Douglas Hurt, "Dairying in Nineteenth Century Ohio," *Old Northwest* 5:397 (Winter 1979-1980).

19. *Akron Beacon and Republican,* Dec. 18, 1893; *Akron Beacon Journal,* Jan. 23, 1897; Mar. 23, 1898.

20. *Progressive Thought and Dawn of Equity,* Feb. 1894; *The Cincinnati Labor Exchange: A Brief Synopsis* (Cincinnati: n.p., n.d.), pp. 2-3; *Cleveland Citizen,* Feb. 1, 1896.

21. *The Cincinnati Labor Exchange,* pp. 3-6.

22. Ibid., p. 8; *Progressive Thought and Dawn of Equity,* July 1894.

23. *The Cincinnati Labor Exchange,* pp. 7-9.

24. *Progressive Thought and Dawn of Equity,* Summer [Aug.] supp., 1898.

25. *The Toledo Labor Exchange: Where It Originated: Its Aims and Objects: What It Proposes to Do for Labor* (Toledo, n.p., n.d.), Samuel M. Jones to Carroll Wright, June 15, 1897, Samuel M. Jones Papers, Ohio Historical Society, Columbus (hereafter cited as OHS).

26. *The Toledo Labor Exchange;* Labor Exchange Papers, Toledo-Lucas County Public Library, Toledo (hereafter cited as TLCPL).

27. Ibid., Jones to William Galliers, May 10, 1897, Samuel M. Jones Papers, OHS.

28. W. C. Hopkins to H. V. Caton, Nov. 15, 1898, Labor Exchange Papers, TLCPL; *Progressive Thought and Dawn of Equity,* Summer [Aug.] supp., 1898.

29. Ibid., June, Oct. 1897.

30. *Akron Beacon Journal,* Jan. 23, June 23, 1897.

31. Ibid., Apr. 14, Aug. 14, 1897.

32. Ibid., July 21, Aug. 14, 1897.

33. Ibid., Oct. 13, Dec. 8, 1897; Mar. 23, 1898.

34. *The Labor Exchange of Akron, Ohio* (Akron, n.p., n.d.).

35. G. B. De Bernardi, *Labor Exchange Fact Book* (Independence, Mo.: Labor Exchange Publications, 1896), p. 12.

36. W. C. Hopkins to H. V. Caton, Nov. 15, 1898, Labor Exchange Papers, TLCPL.

37. De Bernardi, *Colonizing in a Great City* (Independence, Mo.: Labor Exchange Publications, 1897), pp. 2, 5; Bernard J. Brommel, "Debs' Cooperative Commonwealth Plan for Workers," *Labor History* 12:560–69 (Fall 1971); *Progressive Thought and Dawn of Equity,* July 1894; July 1897.

38. *The Story of the Labor Exchange* (n.p.), pp. 3–4.

39. *Progressive Thought and Dawn of Equity,* Sept. 1896.

40. Ibid.

41. Ibid., Apr. 1897; June 1900; *The Story of the Labor Exchange,* p. 13.

42. *Progressive Thought and Dawn of Equity,* Apr. 1897; Sept.–Oct. 1899.

43. Ibid., Sept.–Oct. 1898.

44. *The Story of the Labor Exchange,* pp. 15–17; John W. Fitzgerald to Ignatius Donnelly, May 5, 1899, Ignatius Donnelly Papers, Minnesota Historical Society, St. Paul. *Fort Scott* (Kans.) *Weekly Tribune,* Nov. 8, 1900; Nov. 6, 1902; Nov. 10, 1904.

45. Twelfth Census of Population (1900), Freedom Township, Bourbon County, Kans.; *Progressive Thought and Dawn of Equity,* Sept.–Oct. 1900; *Fulton* (Kans.) *Independent,* Jan. 3, Jan. 10, Mar. 21, Oct. 3, 1902; *Fort Scott Weekly Tribune,* Jan. 9, 1902.

46. *Southern Mercury* (Dallas), Dec. 24, 1896; *Progressive Thought and Dawn of Equity,* June 1895.

47. *Cleveland Citizen,* July 25, 1896.

48. *Progressive Thought and Dawn of Equity,* Mar. 1896; *The Story of the Labor Exchange,* pp. 21–22; E. Z. Ernst, *The Organizer's Guide to the Labor Exchange* (Olathe, Kans.: Labor Exchange Publications, 1895), p. 23.

49. See Roy Rosenzweig, "Radicals and the Jobless: The Musterites and the Unemployed Leagues, 1932-1936," *Labor History* 16:52–77 (Winter 1975).

CHAPTER THREE

1. *Cleveland Citizen,* Oct. 6, 1894; Solon J. Buck, *The Granger Movement: A Study of Agricultural Organization and Its Political, Economic, and Social Manifestations, 1870-1880* (Cambridge, Mass.: Harvard University Press, 1913); D. Sven Nordin, *Rich Harvest: A History of the Grange, 1867-1900* (Jackson: University Press of Mississippi, 1974); Spencer L. Kimball, *Insurance and Public Policy* (Madison: University of Wisconsin Press, 1960), p. 45.

2. Robert C. McMath, Jr., *Populist Vanguard: A History of the Southern Farmers' Alliance* (New York: Norton, Norton Library, 1977), pp. 19–20.

3. Joseph G. Knapp, *The Rise of American Cooperative Enterprises, 1620-1920* (Danville, Ill.: Interstate, 1969), pp. 57–68; Theodore Saloutos, *Farmer Movements in the South, 1865-1933* (Berkeley: University of California Press, 1960), pp. 88–101; McMath, *Populist Vanguard,* pp. 48–63.

4. Knapp, *The Rise of American Cooperative Enterprises,* pp. 79–81, 237–43; *Fort Dodge* (Iowa) *Messenger,* Mar. 21, 1891; *Co-operation* (University Park, Colo.), Sept. 1895.

5. *Sheridan* (Mo.) *Advance,* Feb. 25, 1897; *Ohio Farmer,* Spring, 1896.

6. *Grant County* (S. Dak.) *Review,* Apr. 19, 1894.

7. Ibid., Mar. 12, 1896.

8. *Co-operative News,* ca. 1893, in Jacob S. Coxey Papers, Ohio Historical Society, Columbus (hereafter cited as OHS); *Dubuque* (Iowa) *Daily Times,* Feb. 7, 1893.

9. Melton Alonza McLaurin, *The Knights of Labor in the South* (Westport, Conn.: Greenwood, 1978), pp. 113-14, 123-29; *Dubuque Daily Times,* May 20, 1887.

10. William D. P. Bliss, ed., *Encyclopedia of Social Reform,* s.v. "Rochdale Pioneers"; George Jacob Holyoake, *The History of the Rochdale Pioneers* (n.p., n.d.).

11. *New York World,* Aug. 24, 1894.

12. Hamilton Gardner, "Communism Among the Mormons," *Quarterly Journal of Economics* 38:134-74 (Nov. 1922); Joseph A. Geddes, *The United Order Among the Mormons* (New York: Columbia University Press, 1922); John H. Evans, *Joseph Smith, An American Prophet* (New York: Macmillan, 1933), pp. 241-48; O. Kendall White, Jr., "Mormon Resistance and Accommodation: From Communitarian Socialism to Corporate Capitalism," in *Self-Help in Urban America: Patterns of Minority Economic Development,* National University Publications, Interdisciplinary Urban Series, Scott Cummings, ed. (Port Washington, N.Y.: Kennikat, 1980), pp. 89-112.

13. *Chicago Daily Inter-Ocean,* Aug. 1, 1894.

14. Mark P. Leone, *Roots of Modern Mormonism* (Cambridge, Mass.: Harvard University Press, 1979), pp. 43-85.

15. Leonard J. Arrington and Davis Bitton, *The Mormon Experience: A History of the Latter-Day Saints* (New York: Knopf, 1979), p. 281; *Integral Co-operator* (Enterprise, Kans.), Oct. 1893.

16. *Cleveland Leader,* Mar. 27, 1894; *Cleveland Citizen,* Apr. 14, Apr. 28, 1894; Leslie Seldon Hough, "The Turbulent Spirit: Violence and Coaction among Cleveland Workers, 1877-1899" (Ph.D. diss., University of Virginia, 1977), pp. 177-79.

17. Timothy L. Miller, "Max S. Hayes: A Study of Labor and Socialism" (M.A. thesis, The University of Akron, 1977), pp. 4-9, 13-14; *Cleveland Citizen,* Oct. 6, 1894, supp.

18. Ibid., Nov. 11, 1893; *The Cleveland Industrial Co-operative Society: What We Are* (Cleveland: n.p., 1896), pp. 2-4.

19. Ibid.; *Cleveland Citizen,* Oct. 6, 1894; Jan. 18, 1896.

20. *The Cleveland Industrial Co-operative Society,* pp. 6-7; *Cleveland Citizen,* July 16, 1898.

21. John McVey to Ignatius Donnelly, Feb. 2, 1897, Ignatius Donnelly Papers, Minnesota Historical Society, St. Paul (hereafter cited as MHS).

22. Burkbeck to Jacob S. Coxey, May 11, 1898, Jacob S. Coxey Papers, OHS.

23. *Progressive Thought and Dawn of Equity* (Olathe, Kans.), Jan.-Feb. 1898.

24. *Cleveland Citizen,* 1898-1902.

25. Hayes to Jacob S. Coxey, Mar. 15, 1903, Jacob S. Coxey Papers, OHS.

26. *Review of Reviews* 13:617 (May 1896).

27. *The Hard Times Supply Company* (St. Paul: n.p., 1896), p. 1; "Minnesota" 13:502; R. G. Dun & Co. Collection, Baker Library, Harvard University Graduate School of Business Administration.

28. *The Hard Times Supply Company,* pp. 1-2; J. C. Hanley to Ignatius Donnelly, May 14, 1896, Ignatius Donnelly Papers, MHS.

29. Ibid.; *St. Paul Globe,* Mar. 2, 1897.

30. *Annual Report of the Hard Times Supply Company*, (n.p., 1897), pp. 1, 3-6.

31. *St. Paul Globe*, Mar. 8, 1896; *Zumbrota* (Minn.) *News*, Feb. 23, Mar. 30, May 25, 1894.

32. Ibid.

33. *Mantorville* (Minn.) *Express*, July 2, 1897; *Annual Report of the Hard Times Supply Company*, (1898), pp. 2-3.

34. *Zumbrota News*, June 2, 1899.

35. "Review of the Farmers' Elevator Company, of Zumbrota, Goodhue Co., Minn." (n.p. 1902), p. iii; *Evening Messenger* (Fort Dodge, Iowa), Apr. 14, 1900.

36. *Zumbrota News*, Nov. 10, Dec. 1, 1896.

37. *Progressive Thought and Dawn of Equity*, June 1895.

38. See Robert Loren Morlan, *Political Prairie Fire: The National Nonpartisan League*, 1915-1922 (Minneapolis: University of Minnesota Press, 1955); Andrew A. Bruce, *Nonpartisan League* (New York: Macmillan, 1921); Larry Remele, "North Dakota's Forgotten Farmers Union, 1913-1920," *North Dakota History* 45:4-21 (Spring 1978).

39. *Co-operation*, June 1900.

40. William R. McBride to Henry Olerich, Jan. 15, 1903, Olerich Papers, in possession of Viola Olerich Storms, Moline, Ill. See also Geo. W. Rives to Samuel M. Jones, Jan. 16, 1899, Samuel M. Jones Papers, OHS, for a similar, yet much earlier, view.

CHAPTER FOUR

1. Alfred D. Chandler, Jr., *The Railroads: The Nation's First Big Business* (New York: Harcourt, Brace & World, 1965); Alfred D. Chandler, Jr., *The Visible Hand: The Managerial Revolution in American Business* (Cambridge, Mass.: Harvard University Press, Belknap Press, 1977), especially Chap. 5; Thomas C. Cochran, *Railroad Leaders, 1845-1900* (Cambridge, Mass.: Harvard University Press, 1953).

2. *The Chicago & North-Western Line* (Chicago, C&NW, 1881), p. 2.

3. Hallie Farmer, "The Railroads and Frontier Populism," *Mississippi Valley Historical Review* 13:387-97 (Dec. 1926); *Annual Report of the Board of Railroad Commissioners of Iowa*, 1886 (Des Moines: State Printer, 1887), pp. 52-53; *Dubuque* (Iowa) *Daily Times*, Sept. 12, 1888; *Iowa State Register* (Des Moines), Apr. 24, Aug. 24, 1887.

4. *Free Press* (Devils Lake, N.Dak.), Feb. 13, 1896.

5. *World Almanac, 1893*, pp. 83-85; Newcomb, "The Progress of Federal Railway Regulation," *Political Science Quarterly* 11:201-21 (June 1896).

6. The reason for a narrow-gauge road, presumably a 3-foot width between the rails rather than the standard 4 feet 8½ inches, was likely cost. Narrow-gauge lines required lighter rolling stock, smaller crossties, less grading, and cheaper bridges and culverts.

7. *Dubuque Daily Times*, June 20, 1883; *Chicago Daily Inter-Ocean*, July 2, 1884.

8. Ray Reynolds, *Cat's Paw Utopia* (private publication, 1972), pp. 13-23; *Integral Co-operator* (Enterprise, Kans.), ca. 1890, Dec. 31, 1891.

9. *Farmer's Railroad* (Drayton, N.Dak.), Feb. 26, 1896 (supp., "We're Building Railroads!); *Integral Co-operator*, June 29, 1893; *Dakota Ruralist* (Huron, S.Dak.), Mar. 23, July 27, 1893; *Varnonia* (Oreg.) *Sentinel*, Sept. 6, 1896; *The Rocky Mountain News* (Denver), Oct. 23, 1897; *Progressive Thought and Dawn of Equity* (Olathe, Kans.), May 1897.

10. Gulf and Inter-State Railway Company [prospectus], Ignatius Donnelly Papers, Minnesota Historical Society, St. Paul (hereafter cited as MHS).

11. *"News of the Gulf & Inter-State"* (Topeka: n.p., 1893), pp. 3–4; *Dakota Ruralist,* Jan. 26, July 6, July 27, 1893; Albert Griffin, "A Revolutionary Railway Company," *Arena* 9:777–82 (May 1894).

12. Ibid., p. 778; *News of the Gulf & Inter-State,* p. 2.

13. Griffin, "A Revolutionary Railway Company," p. 778.

14. Charter of the Gulf and Inter-State Ry., Ignatius Donnelly Papers, MHS.

15. *News of the Gulf & Inter-State,* pp. 7–9.

16. Ibid., p. 19.

17. Ibid., pp. 13–16.

18. *Progressive Thought and Dawn of Equity,* Aug. supp., 1895; Keith L. Bryant, Jr., *Arthur E. Stilwell: Promoter with a Hunch* (Nashville: Vanderbilt University Press, 1971), pp. 114–39. Interestingly, transportation enthusiast Stilwell spent much of his time and resources seeking to realize the dreams of Albert K. Owen and the membership of the Credit Foncier Company who sought to build the Texas, Topolobampo and Pacific Railroad (TT&P). Stilwell early in the twentieth century succeeded in partially constructing a latter-day TT&P, his Kansas City, Mexico and Orient. Instead of opening a line from Topolobampo to Kansas City, he completed only that section from Alpine, Texas, to Wichita, Kansas. See Bryant, *Arthur E. Stilwell,* pp. 169–94.

19. *Iowa State Register,* May 14, 1896.

20. *Iowa Homestead* (Des Moines), May, 1, 1896.

21. *Iowa State Register,* Apr. 18, May 14, 1896.

22. *Progressive Thought and Dawn of Equity,* July 1896; "The American Railway: A People's Railroad," (Des Moines: n.p., 1896), pp. 1–5.

23. *Mason City* (Iowa) *Express,* May 22, Aug. 21, 1896; *Iowa State Register,* Nov. 10, 1896.

24. *Progressive Thought and Dawn of Equity,* Nov. 1896; *Twelfth Annual Report of the Chicago Great Western Railway Company For the Year Ending June 30, 1904* (St. Paul: By the company, 1904). A. B. Stickney, with little industry support, felt that government should assume the rate-making function from the railroads. And he generally thought that rail companies had long been guilty of various acts of corporate arrogance. See A. B. Stickney, *The Railway Problem* (St. Paul: D. D. Merrill, 1891).

25. *The American Railway,* pp. 3, 7–8.

26. *Grand Forks* (N.Dak.) *Daily Herald,* July 5, 1894; *Farmer's Railroad* (Cavalier, N.Dak.), June 18, 1894; *Ward County Reporter* (Minot, N.Dak.), Feb. 8, 1895.

27. U.S. Department of the Interior, Twelfth Census of the United States, 1900, T-623-1227, sheet 9; *Farmer's Railroad* (Cavalier), June 18, 1894; ibid. (Drayton), Jan. 8, 1896; *Free Press,* Mar. 5, 1896; *Cavalier County Republican* (Langdon, N.Dak.), Nov. 11, Nov. 18, 1926.

28. *Farmer's Railroad* (Drayton), Aug. 12, 1896.

29. Ibid. (Cavalier), June 18, 1894; newspaper clippings, ca. 1927, File 96, North Dakota Institute for Regional Studies, Fargo.

30. *Farmer's Railroad* (Drayton), Jan. 1, Feb. 26, 1896; ibid. (Cavalier), June 18, 1894.

31. Marion H. Herriot, "Steamboat Transportation on the Red River," *Minnesota History* 21:245–71 (Sept. 1940); F. Stewart Mitchell, "The Chicago, Milwaukee & St. Paul Railway and James J. Hill in Dakota Territory, 1879–1885," *North Dakota History* 47:11–19 (Fall 1980): Raymond H. Merritt, *Creativity, Conflict & Controversy: A History of the St. Paul District U.S. Army Corps of Engineers* (Washington, D.C.: Government Printing Office, 1979), pp. 224–28.

32. *Farmer's Railroad* (Cavalier), June 25, 1894.

33. Elwyn B. Robinson, *History of North Dakota* (Lincoln: University of Nebraska Press, 1966), pp. 217-34; *Fargo* (N.Dak.) *Sun-Independent,* June 3, 1896.

34. Duluth and North Dakota Railroad Company; Articles of Incorporation, in Records of North Dakota Corporations, Book 3 of Domestic Corporations, State Historical Society of North Dakota, Bismarck.

35. *Farmer's Railroad* (Drayton), Sept. 25, 1895; Lawrence Goodwyn, *Democratic Promise: The Populist Moment in America* (New York: Oxford University Press, 1976), pp. 351-86.

36. *Farmer's Railroad* (Drayton), Sept. 25, 1895; June 3, Oct. 28, 1896; *Duluth Evening Herald,* Nov. 21, 1895; *Railroad Gazette* 27:523 (Aug. 2, 1895).

37. *Grafton* (N.Dak.) *Herald-News and Times,* Jan. 16, Feb. 13, 1896; *Farmer's Railroad* (Drayton), Apr. 8, 1896.

38. Ibid., Sept. 11, 1895.

39. *Duluth Commonwealth,* Oct. 15, 1895; *Farmer's Railroad* (Drayton), Oct. 25, 1895; Frank B. Tracy, "The Farmer's Railroad," *McClure's Magazine* 12:35-42 (May 1899); *Milton* (N.Dak.) *Globe,* May 4, 1899; *Grand Forks Daily Herald,* Jan. 21, 1900.

40. *Milton Globe,* Feb. 25, Mar. 4, Mar. 11, Oct. 7, Nov. 18, 1909; *Grand Forks Daily Herald,* Apr. 10, Aug. 14, 1909.

41. *Farmer's Railroad* (Drayton), Jan. 8, 1896.

42. Ibid., special supp., n.d. While not a self-help triumph of the 1890s, a Hines-like venture appeared in southwestern Iowa early in the twentieth century. Transportation-starved farmers in Audubon, Cass, Montgomery, and Shelby counties pooled their capital and labor to build the fifty-five-mile Atlantic Northern and Southern Railroad. The initial segment opened in 1907 between Atlantic and the thriving Danish settlement of Kimballton; three years later the final stretch was completed between Atlantic and Villisca. While the latter trackage was abandoned in 1914 at a considerable financial loss, the former, original piece operated at a modest profit until it was retired in the mid-1930s. See Ben Hur Wilson, "Abandoned Railroads of Iowa," *Iowa Journal of History and Politics* 26:23-25 (Jan. 1928); *History of Grant, Iowa and Douglas Township* (Grant, Iowa: n.p.), pp. 61-64; *Oelwein* (Iowa) *Daily Register,* Sept. 10, 1935.

43. William B. Hennessy, *History of North Dakota* (Bismarck: Bismarck Tribune, 1910), pp. 428-29; *Farmer's Railroad* (Drayton), Feb. 26, 1896, supp.

44. Corporate History, Farmers' Grain & Shipping Company Papers, Great Northern Collection, Minnesota Historical Society, St. Paul (hereafter cited as FG&SCo Papers); Accounting Report on Farmers' Grain and Shipping Company, ibid.; Jos. M. Kelly to F. W. Wilder, October 24, 1900, ibid.; *Free Press,* June 27, 1901, June 18, 1903.

45. Corporate History, FG&SCo Papers; Accounting Report on Farmers' Grain and Shipping Company, ibid.; Jos. M. Kelly to James J. Hill, Sept. 18, 1902, ibid.

46. *Free Press,* Oct. 21.

47. Articles of Incorporation, FG&SCo Papers.

48. Corporate History, FG&SCo Papers; W. R. Begg to R. I. Farrington, May 12, 1905; ibid.; R. I. Farrington to W. R. Begg, Sept. 23, 1907, ibid.

49. Accounting Report on Farmers' Grain and Shipping Company, FG&SCo Papers.

50. *Starkweather* (N.Dak.) *Times,* clippings, n.d., FG&SCo Papers.

51. Securities Farmers' Grain & Shipping Company, FG&SCo Papers; *Devils Lake* (N.Dak.) *Journal,* June 9, June 30, 1905.

52. Accounting Report on Farmers' Grain and Shipping Company, FG&SCo Papers.

53. *Devils Lake Journal,* Nov. 6, Nov. 11, 1905; Remarks of Hon. H. C. Hansbrough, FG&SCo Papers.

54. Accounting Report on Farmers' Grain and Shipping Company, FG&SCo Papers.

55. Gray to R. I. Farrington, June 1, 1912, FG&SCo Papers.

56. "Varnish" is a commonly used term to refer to passenger trains. In an era before all-steel equipment, roads employed wooden cars, often with oak exteriors and highly polished mahogany and walnut interiors; hence the expression. Superb summaries of the advantages of having the FG&SCo as an affiliated concern are found in G. R. Martin to J. M. Kelly, May 10, 1920, FG&SCo Papers, and Jos. M. Kelly to R. I. Farrington, Nov. 26, 1910, ibid.

57. Right of Way, Land & Tax Comm'r. to G. R. Martin, Nov. 11, 1924, FG&SCo Papers; Jos. M. Kelly to R. I. Farrington, Jan. 22, 1908, ibid.

58. Jos. M. Kelly to "Dear Sir," June 14, 1902, FG&SCo Papers; *Devils Lake Journal,* Dec. 22, 1905; R. I. Farrington to J. M. Gruber, May 21, 1909, FG&SCo Papers.

59. The Matter of Rates on the Farmers' Line, n.d., FG&SCo Papers; L. Willard Jones to Jos. M. Kelly, Oct. 1, 1909, ibid.

60. Jos. M. Kelly to R. I. Farrington, Aug. 14, 1905, FG&SCo Papers; Pennington to L. W. Hill, Sept. 25, 1904, ibid.

61. H. A. Wallis to Louis W. Hill, Apr. 19, 1909, FG&SCo Papers; Jos. M. Kelly to L. W. Hill, Apr. 11, 1910, ibid.; Jos. M. Kelly to L. W. Hill, Aug. 24, 1912; U.S. Interstate Commerce Commission, Finance Docket No. 14276, Oct. 26, 1943, ibid.

62. Turner, "Understanding the Populists," *Journal of American History* 67: 354-73 (Sept. 1980).

63. Efforts also occurred during the depression to launch consumer-owned barge service along various internal waterways, particularly the Ohio and Mississippi River systems. Little is known about such ventures, but they were classic self-help experiments. One firm that called itself the "People's Own Boat Line," started at Dubuque, Iowa, in April 1894, boasted "That it is cutting rates by a quarter [over investor-owned lines] . . . [and] it shows what can be done when shippers do their bit by turning to their own powers." The concern, with its single towboat and three barges, failed by the late nineties. See *Dubuque Daily Times,* Apr. 27, 1894; Aug. 10, 1896.

64. *Altrurian* (Denver), Jan. 1895.

65. *Progressive Thought and Dawn of Equity,* Aug. supp. 1895.

66. George W. Hilton and John F. Due, *The Electric Interurban Railways in America* (Stanford, Calif.: Stanford University Press, 1960), pp. 4-15; *Dictionary of American Biography,* s.v. "Sprague, Frank Julian."

67. George H. Gibson, "High-Speed Electric Interurban Railways," *Annual Report of the Board of Regents of the Smithsonian Institution* (Washington, D.C.: Government Printing Office, 1904), p. 311; Guy Morrison Waler, *The Why and How of Interurban Railways* (Chicago: n.p., 1904), pp. 3-4; Hilton and Due, *The Electric Interurban Railways in America,* p. 8.

68. James Glen, "The Interurban Trolley Flyers," *World's Work* 13:8406-7 (Jan. 1907); "The Farmer and the Interurban," *Street Railway Journal* 28:497 (Oct. 6, 1906).

69. One reform organ, the labor exchange's *Progressive Thought and Dawn of Equity,* noted in its supplement for Winter 1896 that farmer traction systems were

being actively considered in six states, New York, Ohio, Indiana, Wisconsin, Minnesota, and California, and that "electricity and not steam could well be the best solution to the transportation problem."

70. Hilton and Due, *The Electric Interurban Railways in America,* p. 255; *Breeder's Gazette* 25:ii (Aug. 1895).

71. *Farmer's Railroad* (Drayton), May 20, 1896; Hilton and Due, *The Electric Interurban Railways in America,* pp. 9-10, 76, 267.

72. Ibid., pp. 10-11, 267; *Progressive Thought and Dawn of Equity,* Jan.-Feb. 1901.

73. H. Roger Grant, "Electric Traction Promotion in the South Iowa Coalfields," *The Palimpsest* 58:23-27 (Jan.-Feb. 1977). The best illustration of a successful farmers' interurban was the Minnesota Northwestern Electric Traction Company that operated eighteen miles of trackage between Thief River Falls and Goodridge. Opened in 1914, this carrier functioned until 1940. See "A Farmers Railway Is Built," FG&SCo Papers; Hilton and Due, *The Electric Interurban Railways in America,* p. 358.

74. *Farmer's Railroad* (Drayton), n.d., clippings in FG&SCo Papers.

75. Ibid., Feb. 26, 1896 supp.

CHAPTER FIVE

1. W. W. Williams to Henry Olerich, Jan. 28, 1894, in Henry Olerich Papers, in possession of Viola Olerich Storms, Moline, Ill. (hereafter cited as Olerich Papers).

2. See Robert S. Fogarty, "American Communes, 1865-1914," *Journal of American Studies* 9:145-62 (Aug. 1975); Charles Pierce LeWarne, "Labor and Communitarianism, 1880-1900," *Labor History* 16:393-407 (Summer 1975).

3. *Phalanx,* Apr. 1, 1844.

4. Jacob Beilhart, *Life and Teachings* (Burbank, Calif.: Freedom Hill Pressery, 1925), p. 75. See also Jacob Beilhart, *Anarchy, Its Causes, and a Suggestion for Its Cure* (n.p., n.d.).

5. *Altrurian* (Denver), Summer supp., 1895.

6. *Rocky Mountain News* (Denver), Nov. 1, 1897; Charles Pierce LeWarne, "Equality Colony: The Plan to Socialize Washington," *Pacific Northwest Quarterly* 59:137-46 (July 1968); Wilbur S. Shepperson, *Retreat to Nevada: A Socialist Colony of World War I* (Reno: University of Nevada Press, 1966), pp. 60-104.

7. Edward Bellamy, *Looking Backward, 2000-1887* (Boston: Ticknor, 1888); William Dean Howells, *A Traveler from Altruria* (New York: Harper and Brothers, 1894); Edward B. Payne, "Altruria," *American Magazine of Civics* 6:168-71 (Feb. 1895); Morrison I. Swift, "Altruria in California," *Overland Monthly* 19:643-45 (June 1897); Robert V. Hine, *California's Utopian Colonies* (New Haven: Yale University Press, 1966), 101-13. See also Kenneth M. Roemer, "Sex Roles, Utopia and Change: The Family in Late 19th Century Utopian Literature," *American Studies* 13:33-47 (Fall 1972).

8. See Kenneth M. Roemer, *The Obsolete Necessity: America in Utopian Writings, 1885-1900* (Kent, Ohio: Kent State University Press, 1976); and Allyn B. Forbes, "The Literary Quest for Utopia, 1888-1900," *Social Forces* 6:179-89 (Dec. 1927).

9. Frank Hall, *History of the State of Colorado . . . from 1858 to 1890,* 2d ed. (Chicago: Blakely Printing Company, 1895), 4:497.

10. Ibid., Charles W. Caryl, *New Era: Presenting the Plans for the New Era Union to Help Develop and Utilize the Best Resources of This Country* (private publication, 1897), p. 61.

11. Hall, *History of the State of Colorado,* 4:497; *Philadelphia Press,* Feb. 20, 1893.

12. Charles W. Caryl, *A Brief History of the Movement to Abolish the Slums of Philadelphia* (Philadelphia: n.p., 1893), pp. 9, 18, 24; Harland B. Phillips, "A War on Philadelphia's Slums: Walter Vrooman and the Conference of Moral Workers, 1893," *Pennsylvania Magazine of History and Biography* 76:47-62 (Jan. 1952).

13. Ibid., pp. 49, 60-61; Ross E. Paulson, *Radicalism and Reform: The Vrooman Family and American Social Thought* (Lexington: University of Kentucky Press, 1968), pp. 89-90.

14. *Colorado Springs Mining Investor,* Apr. 9, 1898; *Rocky Mountain News,* Aug. 3, 1898; *Boulder* (Colo.) *Camera,* Aug. 21, 1959; *Ores and Metals* 6:10-13 (July 1897).

15. Copies of the first edition of *The New Era* were typed. In 1897 Caryl had published the book in an expanded form: *New Era: Presenting the Plans for the New Era Union to Help Develop and Utilize the Best Resources of This Country.* This version is the source used in this chapter. Arno Press in New York reprinted this edition in 1971 as part of its "Utopian Literature Series."

16. *Integral Co-operator* (Enterprise, Kans.), Apr. 7, 1892.

17. Ibid.

18. Caryl to Henry Olerich, June 15, 1896, Olerich Papers.

19. Caryl, *New Era,* pp. 30-90.

20. Ibid., p. 105.

21. Ibid., p. 134; Caryl to Olerich, June 15, 1896.

22. Caryl, *New Era,* pp. 134-36.

23. Ibid., pp. 120, 141.

24. Charles W. Caryl to Hazen S. Pingree, Dec. 11, 1896, Hazen S. Pingree Papers, Burton Historical Collection, Detroit Public Library (hereafter cited as BHC).

25. Edward L. Gallatin, *What Life Has Taught Me* (Denver: J. Frederic, 1900), pp. 94, 97.

26. *Altrurian* (Piñon, Colo.), Nov. 1897; *Colorado Springs Mining Investor,* Apr. 9, 1898; *New Time* (St. Louis), Feb. 1898; *Denver Times,* Aug. 16, 1899; Apr. 8, 1902; Feb. 21, 1903; *Ores and Metals* 6:15-16 (Sept. 1901); *Rocky Mountain Daily News,* Feb. 6, Feb. 11, 1912; *Denver Post,* Feb. 14, 1912.

27. *Progressive Thought and Dawn of Equity* (Olathe, Kans.), Feb. 12, 1894; Olerich to Jack W. Wilson, Jan. 26, 1896, Olerich Papers.

28. *Twentieth Century Farmer* (Los Angeles), Apr. 1894; *Dakota Ruralist* (Huron, S.Dak.), Nov. 29, 1894; *Co-operation* (University Park, Colo.), Sept. 1894; *Cleveland Citizen,* July 27, 1895; *Fulton* (Kans.) *Independent,* Feb. 17, 1899; Frederick de L. Booth Tucker, "The Farm Colonies of the Salvation Army," *Forum* 23:750-60 (Aug. 1897); *Nation* 64:467 (June 24, 1897); Eugene Higgins to Samuel M. Jones, Dec. 18, 1897, Samuel M. Jones Papers, Ohio Historical Society, Columbus (hereafter cited as OHS); Samuel M. Jones to Rev. B. Fay Mills, May 3, 1898, ibid.

29. *Iowa State Register* (Des Moines), Feb. 5, 1895; *Altrurian* (Denver), Summer supp., 1895.

30. *Black Hills Weekly Journal* (Rapid City, S.Dak.), Nov. 26, 1896.

31. Ibid.

32. Ibid., *Progressive Thought and Dawn of Equity,* Jan. supp., 1897.

33. O. Gene Clanton, *Kansas Populism: Ideas and Men* (Lawrence: University Press of Kansas, 1969), pp. 185-206; Breidenthal to Henry Olerich, Jan. 5, 1897, Olerich Papers.

34. Robert S. Fogarty, *Dictionary of American Communal and Utopian History* (Westport, Conn.: Greenwood, 1980), pp. 127, 134-36, 139-40, 161-62; Ralph

Albertson, *A Survey of Mutualistic Communistic Communities in America* (New York: AMS Press, 1973; orig. pub. 1936); Will Alfred Hinds, *American Communities and Cooperative Colonies* (Chicago: Charles H. Kerr, 1908); Alexander Kent, "Co-operative Communities in the United States," *United States Department of Labor Bulletin* 35:563–646 (July 1909); Frederick A. Bushee, "Communistic Societies in the United States," *Political Science Quarterly* 20:625–64 (Dec. 1905), Howard H. Quint, "Julius A. Wayland, Pioneer Socialist Propagandist," *Mississippi Valley Historical Review* 35:587–93: *Altrurian* (Denver), Aug. 1896; ibid. (Piñon, Colo.), Nov. 1897.

35. Charles Pierce LeWarne, *Utopias on Puget Sound, 1885-1915* (Seattle: University of Washington Press, 1975), pp. 55–113; Paul and Blanche Alyea, *Fairhope, 1894-1954: The Story of a Single Tax Colony* (University: University of Alabama Press, 1956); John D. Fish, "The Christian Commonwealth Colony: A Georgia Experiment, 1896–1900," *Georgia Historical Quarterly* 57:213–25 (Summer 1973); *The Preamble Constitution and By-Laws of the Christian Co-operative Association* (Clay Center, Kans., 1899).

36. *Altrurian* (Denver, Colo.), Summer supp., 1895.

37. Wayland to Henry Olerich, Nov. 1, 1896, Olerich Papers. See also John Egerton, *Visions of Utopia: Nashoba, Rugby, Ruskin, and the "New" Communities in Tennessee's Past*, (Knoxville: University of Tennessee Press, 1977), pp. 64–86; "The Co-operative Colony at Ruskin," *American Monthly Review of Reviews* 16:606–7 (Nov. 1897).

38. *Co-operation*, Sept. 1895; Ralph Albertson, "The Christian Commonwealth in Georgia," *Georgia Historical Quarterly* 29:131 (June 1945).

39. *Rocky Mountain News,* Oct. 31, 1897; *Spokane Chronicle,* ca. 1895, clipping in Olerich Papers.

40. *Altrurian* (Denver), Summer supp., 1895; Joseph A. Johnson to Henry Olerich, July 11, 1896, Olerich Papers.

41. *Social Gospel* (Commonwealth, Ga.) Mar. 1898; George Howard Gibson to Henry Olerich, May 5, 1898 [?], Olerich Papers.

42. Department of Commerce and Labor, Bureau of the Census, *Twelfth Census of the United States Taken in the Year 1900,* Wilson Township, Dallas County, Mo.; *Communist* (St. Louis), Aug. 1871.

43. Ibid.

44. Hal D. Sears, "Alcander Longley, Missouri Communist: A History of Reunion Community and a Study of the Constitution of Reunion and Friendship," *Bulletin of the Missouri Historical Society* 25:123–31 (Jan. 1969); *Communist* (Buffalo, Mo.), Apr. 1872.

45. Ibid. (Friendship Community, Mo.), Aug. 1872; Mar. 1875; *Missouri Democrat* (St. Louis), Aug. 11, 1872; *Buffalo* (Mo.). *Reflex,* June 6, 1873; Deed Record Book F, Dallas County, Mo., p. 505.

46. Hinds, *American Communities,* pp. 403–4; Bennett to Henry Olerich, July 2, 1895, Olerich Papers.

47. Ibid., "Prospectus of the Home Employment Co-operative Company" (1901).

48. Kent, "Co-operative Communities in the United States," p. 634; *Buffalo Reflex,* Mar. 7, 1902.

49. Mrs. Oliver Howard, State Historical Society of Missouri, to author, Mar. 13, 1973; Bennett to Henry Olerich, May 1, 1903, Olerich Papers.

50. Hinds, *American Communities,* p. 404. James D. Attebery to author, Feb. 3, 1972. William Bennett's HECC dissolved sometime between 1904 and 1906. No "obituary" for the colony appeared in the area press, but land records reveal that the Bennetts liquidated their Long Lane holdings during this time. According to an elderly resident, "They moved to Arkansas." The colony's long abandoned store

building and Bennett's primitive log cabin on the nearby farm are the only tangible remains of this Ozark pragmatist utopia. See Deed Record Book 51, Dallas County, Mo., pp. 534-35; ibid., Book 60, p. 320; ibid., Book 61, p. 40; ibid., Book 64, p. 525; ibid., Book 67, p. 25; James D. Attebery to Dorothy J. Caldwell, July 1960, State Historical Society of Missouri Papers, Columbia.

51. C. E. Smith, *A Brief History of the Colorado Co-operative Company* (Denver, n.p.), pp. 1-3; Gallatin, *What Life Has Taught Me,* p. 65.

52. *Altrurian* (Denver), Jan., Feb. 1895.

53. Prospectus of the Colorado Co-operative Company (n.d.), pp. 1-2; Articles of Incorporation (No. 16614), Feb. 16, 1894; Colorado Secretary of State, Denver, pp. 54; *Altrurian* (Denver), Aug. 1895; William D. P. Bliss, ed., *New Encyclopeida of Social Reform* 3d ed., s.v. "Colorado Co-operative Company."

54. *Altrurian* (Denver), Summer supp. 1895; ibid. (Piñon, Colo.), Apr. 1898; *Progressive Thought and Dawn of Equity,* Jan. supp. 1897.

55. "Cooperative Colony-Builders," *Out West* 19:108-14; Ellen Z. Peterson, "Origins of the Town of Nucla," *Colorado Magazine* 26:253 (Oct. 1949).

56. Wilson Rockwell, "Uncompahgre Frontier," State Historical Society of Colorado Library, pp. 134-35; Frances M. Croke, "A History of the Colorado Co-operative Colony, and the Town of Nucla," ibid., pp. 7-8; Hinds, *American Communities,* p. 501.

57. Duane D. Mercer, "The Colorado Co-operative Company, 1894-1904," *Colorado Magazine* 44:297-98; *Rocky Mountain Sentinel* (Denver), ca. 1895.

58. *Altrurian* (Denver), Jan. 1895; C. E. Julihu, "Pinon—A New Brook Farm of the West," *National Magazine* 11:33-34 (Oct. 1899).

59. *Integral Co-operator,* Apr. 1, 1894; *Co-operation,* Oct. 1894; *Denver Times,* July 18, 1894; July 15, 1898; June 27, 1899.

60. Gallatin, *What Life Has Taught Me,* p. 56.

61. *Nucla: City of the Future* (n.p., n.d.); *Altrurian* (Piñon, Colo.), Nov. 29, 1899; *Progressive Thought and Dawn of Equity,* Mar.-Apr. 1904.

62. *Nucla:* pp. 3-4, 8.

63. Mercer, "The Colorado Co-operative Company," pp. 305-6; *Denver Times,* Mar. 7, 1900; *Denver Republican,* June 24, 1900; *Appeal to Reason* (Girard, Kans.), June 13, 1903; Ernest Wooster, *Communities Past and Present* (New Llano, La.: Llano Colonist, 1924), p. 62.

64. Mrs. Lloyd R. Jacobson to author, July 25, 1973.

AFTERWORD

1. *Wall Street Journal,* Apr. 21, 1980; Clark Kerr, "Productive Enterprises of the Unemployed" (Ph.D. diss., University of California, 1939); Edward Ainsworth Williams, *Federal Aid for Relief* (New York: Columbia University Press, 1939); *Detroit Free Press,* May 7, 1933.

2. *Life Begins the Day You Start a Garden* (Burlington, Vt.: n.p., 1979); *Community Gardening* (Burlington, Vt.: n.p., 1977); *Wall Street Journal,* Dec. 11, 1980; "Gardening: A Blooming Boom," *Newsweek* 89:86-88 (June 11, 1979).

3. See *Detroit Free Press,* May 9, 1980; *Michigan Chronicle* (Detroit), May 10, 1980; *Detroit Legal News,* Apr. 27, 1981.

4. Peggy Rand to author, Jan. 25, 1980.

5. Ibid.; "Senior Gleaners: A Statement of Purpose."

6. *Wall Street Journal,* Sept. 18, 1980; *Akron Beacon Journal,* Dec. 15, 1980.

7. William E. Leverette, "Ralph Borsodi: Urbanite as Agrarian," *Proceedings of the Southeastern American Studies Association* (1979), pp. 66-75; Ralph Borsodi, "What to Do about Inflation," *Green Revolution* 10:13-24 (1972); "The

Nature of Banking," ibid., 34:12-13 (Dec. 1977). See also Ralph Borsodi, *The Distribution Age* (New York: D. Appleton, 1927) and *Flight from the City* (New York: Harper, 1933).

8. "The Exeter Experiment," *Forbes* 113:45 (Feb. 1, 1974).

9. "Paying with Constants instead of Dollars," *Business Week* 2329:29 (May 4, 1974).

10. *Ogden* (Iowa) *Reporter,* Nov. 9, 1933; Elmer G. Powers Diary, Jan. 20, 1933, Division of the State Historical Society, Iowa City.

11. John A. Crampton, *The National Farmers Union: Ideology of a Pressure Group* (Lincoln: University of Nebraska Press, 1965), pp. 34-52; Farmland Industries Annual Report (1979).

12. *Hyde Park* (Chicago) *Herald,* Dec. 3, 1980; Report of the Cooperative League of the USA (1980).

13. "California Co-op Cuts Bills in Half," *Aging* 274:3-5 (Aug. 1977).

14. *Poor's Manual of Railroads* (New York: Poor's, 1919), p. 2073; *Oelwein* (Iowa) *Daily Register,* Aug. 31, 1948.

15. *Modern Railroads,* Oct. 3, 1980.

16. "The Big Rush into Short-line Railroads," *Business Week* 2302:104-5 (Oct. 20, 1973); "Bought a Railroad," *Successful Farming,* pp. 8-9 (Feb. 1975); Michale M. Bartels to author, Sept. 20, 1980.

17. *Cleveland Plain Dealer,* June 15, 1977; *New York Times,* Oct. 3, 1971. See also Robert Houriet, *Getting Back Together* (New York: Coward-McCann & Geoghegan, 1971).

18. *New York Times,* Dec. 1, Dec. 3, 1980; Richard Fairfield, *Communes USA: A Personal Tour* (Baltimore: Penguin Books, 1972), pp. 334-44.

19. *Akron Beacon Journal,* Apr. 11, 1971; Arthur Peterson to author, Aug. 2, 1975.

20. *New York Times,* Feb. 17, 1973; Nov. 20, 1975; Laurence R. Veysey, *The Communal Experience: Anarchist and Mystical Counter-Cultures in America* (New York: Harper and Row, 1973); Richard Mills, *Young Outsiders: A Study of Alternative Communities* (New York: Pantheon Books, 1973).

21. Borsodi, "The Nature of Banking," p. 12; Donovan L. Hofsommer to author, July 3, 1980; *New York Times,* Mar. 4, 1977.

22. John Anderson to author, Jan. 5, 1981.

23. "Self-Service," *New Republic* 183:14-15 (Nov. 15, 1980); *New York Times,* Mar. 4, 1977.

# Index

AGRI Industries, 135
Akron, Ohio, 48. *See also* Labor exchange(s)
Albertson, Ralph, 115
Albia Interurban Railway, 99
Allotment plan (England), 26, 31
Altruria, California, 104, 113
*Altrurian,* 114
American Pacific Railroad, 77–78
American Railway Union, 80
*Arena,* 8
Arkansas, 54, 78
Armourdale, North Dakota, 94
Associated Charities, 32, 36
Association for Improving the Condition of the Poor, 32, 33
Atchison, Topeka and Santa Fé Railroad, 7
Atlantic and Pacific Railway, 135

Baltimore, Maryland, 18–19
Baring Brothers, 5, 104
Barter Systems (Oklahoma City), 131
Beaver, Iowa, 132–33
Beilhart, Jacob, 102
Bellamy, Edward, 45, 103, 104
Bennett, Edward, 117
Bennett, Emily, 117
Bennett, William H., 116–19
Biddle, William Henry, 112
Borsodi, Ralph, 131–32
Boston, Massachusetts, 15, 31, 112
Brandon, Devils Lake and Southern Railway, 92
*Breeder's Gazette,* 97
Breidenthal, John W., 112, 113
Brisbane, Albert, 102
*Brockton Times,* 40
Brooklyn, New York, 31, 32
Browne, Carl, 14
Bryan, William Jennings, 12
Buffalo, Missouri, 117
Buffalo, New York, 31
Buford, William, 130
Burkbeck, J. W., 67

California, 129, 134
Camp, H. B., 51, 52
Canadian Pacific Railway, 83, 88, 94

Carlton, Will, 4–5
Caryl, Charles W., 104–11
Cassidy, Mark, 129
*Catholic Worker, The,* 137
Catholic Worker Movement, 136–37
Central Labor Council, 67
Central Relief Committee, 18–19
Central States Traffic Association, 52
*Charities Review,* 23
Chautauqua and North East Grape Association, 60
Chicago, Burlington and Quincy Railroad, 4, 82, 134, 135
Chicago, Illinois, 31, 32, 39, 76, 81, 82, 135
Chicago, Milwaukee and St. Paul Railway, 5, 61, 82, 93, 135
Chicago, Rock Island and Pacific Railway, 82, 135
Chicago and North Western Railway, 5, 82, 135, 136
*Chicago Daily Inter-Ocean,* 64
Chicago Great Western Railway, 82–83
*Chicago Tribune,* 39
Christian Commonwealth, 113, 114, 115
Christian Co-operative Association, 114
Church of Jesus Christ of Latter-Day Saints. *See* Cooperative stores, Mormons
Ciba-Geigy, 139
Cincinnati, Iowa, 8–9
Cincinnati, Ohio, 45. *See also* Labor exchange(s)
*Cityless and Countryless World, A,* 111
Cleveland, Grover, 11–12, 14
Cleveland, Ohio, 65, 98. *See also* Cooperative stores
*Cleveland Citizen,* 16, 66
*Coin's Financial School,* 108
*Colonizing in a Great City,* 53–54
Colorado, 14, 16–17. *See also* Charles W. Caryl; Intentional communities
Colville, Washington, 72
*Commercial and Financial Chronicle,* 3

Community gardens
  assessment of, 37–40
  and "back-to-the-land" concept,
    33–35
  and Detroit, 23–30
  origins of, 25–27
  and single-tax relationship, 35–36
  spread of, 31
  structure of, 27–28, 30–33
  weaknesses of, 39–40
  and work ethic, 36–37, 40
Conference of Moral Workers, 106
*Co-operation,* 72
Co-operative Brotherhood, 113
Cooperative stores
  assessment of, 72–73
  and Cleveland Industrial Co-
    operative Society, 57, 65–68
  and Mormons, 64–65
  origins of, 59–63
  and People's Hard Times Supply
    Company, 68–71
  and Rochdale Plan, 63–64
*Cosmopolitan,* 103
Cotton, Frank W., 54
Coxey, Jacob S., 14–15
Coxey Non-Interest Bond Bill, 14, 47
Credit Foncier Company, 45, 75, 121
Crocker, Uriel H., 10
Crookston, Minnesota, 88

D. M. Ferry Seed Company, 28
*Dakota Ruralist,* 78
Day, Dorothy, 136, 137
De Bernardi, G. B., 41–44, 47, 53–54
Debs, Eugene V., 53, 80, 113
Deer River, Minnesota, 87
Delft, Holland, 31
Delphi, Colorado, 106, 110
Denver, Colorado, 31, 32
Denver Woman's Club, 32
Depression of 1893–1897
  agricultural dislocations of, 3–4, 9,
    48
  and business conditions, 5–8
  charities' response to, 17–19
  and Democratic party, 11–12
  and Europe, 5–6
  federal response to, 11–14
  individual response to, 16–17
  initial response to, 9–11
  misery during, 8–9
  municipal response to, 15
  and Panic of 1893, 3, 6–7
  and People's Party, 12
  and Republican party, 13–14
  states' response to, 15–16
  and unemployment, 8–9, 23, 48, 65
  and work ethic, 19–22
Des Moines, Iowa, 39, 81, 82, 115

Detroit, Michigan, viii, 129–30. *See
    also* Community gardens
*Detroit Evening News,* 28
*Detroit Free Press,* 128
Detroit Water Board, 28
Devils Lake, North Dakota, 89, 90, 93
Devils Lake and Northern Railway,
    90, 91
Dingley Act, 14
Drayton, North Dakota, 85, 87, 88
Drop City, Colorado, 136
Duluth, Minnesota, 83, 84, 87, 88

Egeland, North Dakota, 94
Ellsberry, North Dakota, 92
England, 5, 31, 62
Enterprise Community, 117
Equality Colony, 113
Equity store, 45
Exeter, New Hampshire, 132

Fairhope Industrial Association, 35,
    113, 114, 115
"Farm-A-Lot" Program, 129, 130
"Farm" Colony, 136
Farmers' Alliance, 43–44, 53, 59–60
Farmers' Elevator Company, 70
Farmers' Mercantile and Elevator
    Company, 70, 71, 72
*Farmer's Railroad,* 85, 86, 99
Farmers' railroads
  and American Railway Company,
    81–83
  assessment of, 99–100
  and Duluth and North Dakota
    Railroad, 83–88
  and electric interurbans, 96–99
  and Farmers' Grain and Shipping
    Company, 89–95
  and Gulf and Inter-State Railway,
    78–81
  and "iron road" movement, 95–96
  origins of, 74–77
  structure of, 76
Farmer's Railway, 88
Farmers' Union, 133
Farmland Industries, 133
Fels, Joseph, 36
Fels, Mary, 36
Fitzgerald, John W., 55
Flower, B. O., 40
Fond du Lac, Wisconsin, 11
Food Advisory Service, 134
*Forum,* 19
Fourier, Charles, 102, 118
France, 5
Fremont, Ohio, 98
Friendship Community, 117

Galesburg, Illinois, 31

Gallatin, E. L., 123
Gallery Faire Enterprises, 134
Galveston, Texas, 78
Gardener, Cornelius, 26, 28
Gaskin, Stephen, 136
George, Henry, 35, 114
Germany, 5, 62
Gifford, L. L., 123
Gleaner movement, 130–31
Gold Extraction Mining and Supply
    Company, 106
Goodwyn, Lawrence, 86
Gould, E. R. L., 36–37
Grain Terminal Association, 133
*Grand Forks Daily Herald,* 88
Grange. *See* National Grange of the
    Patrons of Husbandry
*Grant County Review,* 62
Granville, Ohio, 96
Gray, Carl R., 92–93
Great Northern Railway, 84, 85, 86,
    88, 89, 91, 92, 93, 94, 95
Great Plains Railway, 135–36
Green, James T. R. 81, 83

Hale, Edward Everett, 108
Hampton, Iowa, 82, 83
Hanley, J. C., 68, 69
Hannah, North Dakota, 84
Hansboro, North Dakota, 92
Hansbrough, Henry C., 92
Harvey, William H., 108
Hayes, Max S., 65, 66, 67, 68
Helping Hand Society, 19
Hill, James J., 84, 85, 88, 91
Hines, David Wellington ("Farmer"),
    83–84, 85, 86–88
Hiteman, Iowa, 99
Hopkins, Eugene, 125
Hopkins, W. C., 49, 50
Howard, James, 54, 55
Howard, John, 54, 55
Howells, William Dean, 103, 104
Hubbard, Elbert, 20
Humboldt, Saskatchewan, 88

Iler, James, 45
Illinois Midland Railroad, 134–35
Independence, Missouri, 47
Indianapolis, Indiana, 76
*Integral Co-operator,* 65
Intentional communities
    assessment of, 126–27
    before 1893, 103–04
    and colonies of the 1890s, 113–15
    and Colorado Co-operative Com-
        pany, 120–26, 127
    and Home Employment Co-
        operative Company, 116–20
    and paper utopias, 111–12

and permanency, 115–16
    as temporary, 115–16
    types of, 101–03
    and utopian writers, 104–11
Interstate Commerce Commission, 75
Iowa, 8–9, 74–75, 78
Iowa Pioneer Phalanx, 102
*Iowa State Register,* 75

Jones, Fred, 17
Jones, Jim, 136
Jones, Samuel M. ("Golden Rule"),
    16, 22, 49, 50

Kansas, 4, 54–56, 78, 112–13
Kansas City, Missouri, 39, 81
Kansas City, Pittsburg and Gulf
    Railroad, 81
Kansas-Siñaloa Investment Company.
    *See* Credit Foncier Company
Kelly, Harry, 102
Kelly, Joseph M., 90, 91, 92, 94
Kenmare, North Dakota, 93
Killarney, Manitoba, 94
King's Daughters, 19
Kingston, New York, 39
Knights Co-operative Grocery, 63
Knights of Labor, 62–63
Knights of Labor Co-operative Tobac-
    co Company, 63

Labor exchange(s)
    and Akron, Ohio, local, 51–52
    assessment of, 57–58
    and Cincinnati, Ohio, local, 48–49
    efforts to institutionalize, 53–56
    and Freedom Colony, 54–56
    and Maple Colony, 54
    origins of, 41–46
    spread of, 47
    structure of, 43–44
    and Toledo, Ohio, local, 49–50
    weaknesses of, 56–57
Lake Shore and Michigan Southern
    Railway, 98
Lake Shore Electric Railway, 98
Lebanon, Missouri, 119
Leola, South Dakota, 46
Lincoln, Nebraska, 78
Long Island City, New York, 32
Long Island Improvement Company,
    32
Long Lane, Missouri, 117, 119, 120
Longley, Alcander, 117, 118
*Looking Backward,* 45–46, 103
*Los Angeles Times,* 40
Lowell, Josephine S., 21

McKinley Tariff, 14
McMath, Robert J., Jr., 60

McVey, John, 67
Maher, John W., 90, 91
Manitoba, 78, 90
Melfort, Saskatchewan, 88
Michigan, 8. *See also* Community gardens
Michigan Agricultural College, 28
Milbank Co-operative Creamery Association, 61-62
Miller, L. L., 123
Millington, Illinois, 134
Minneapolis, Minnesota, 32, 83, 85
Minnesota, 78. *See also* Cooperative stores
Minnesota State Alliance, 68
Missouri, 8, 78. *See also* Intentional communities
*Missouri Valley Eye,* 37
Monsanto, 139
Morning Star Ranch, California, 136
Moses, E. R., 34-35
Muste, the Reverend A. J., 56

National Association for Gardening, 129
National Cordage Company, 6-7
National Grange of the Patrons of Husbandry, 42, 59, 64
National Irrigation Congress, 34
Nebraska, 4, 9, 45, 78, 135
Nelson, N. O., 68
Nevada, 103
*New Era, The,* 106, 108
New Era Union, 108-11
New Orleans, Louisiana, 76
New York, 8, 17
New York, New York, 8, 31, 32-33, 76, 136
New York Charity Organization Society, 21
*New York Herald,* 22
*New York Times,* 6
*New York Tribune,* 4
*New York World,* 31, 33, 64
Newark, Illinois, 134
Newark, Ohio, 96
Newark Farmers' Grain Cooperative Company, 134
Newcomb, H. T., 75
Newton, the Reverend R. Heber, 62
Non-Partisan League, 72, 73
North Dakota, 72, 73, 75, 78, 84-85, 95. *See also* Farmers' railroads
North Dakota and Minnesota Central Railway, 89
Northern Pacific Railway, 93
Nucla, Colorado. *See* Intentional communities

Ohio, 48, 97, 98. *See also* Cooperative stores; Labor exchange(s)
*Ohio Farmer,* 61
Oklahoma, 9, 78
Olerich, Henry, 69, 111
Oliver Iron and Steel Company, 7
Olmstead, North Dakota, 93
Omaha, Nebraska, 31, 81, 82, 83
*Omaha World-Herald,* 59
O'Neil, P. F., 51
Oskaloosa, Iowa, 115
Owen, Albert Kimsey, 45, 76-77

Pacific City, Siñaloa, Mexico, 77
Padanaram Colony, 137
Paine, Robert Treat, 108
Peffer, William A., 14
Pennington, Edmund, 94
Pennsylvania, 8
People's party, 53, 75, 78, 112-13
People's Railroad of America, 76
People's Temple, 136
Philadelphia, Pennsylvania, 17, 31, 32, 36, 105-6
Philadelphia and Reading Railroad, 6
Pingree, Hazen S., 23-26, 29-30, 140
Pingree, Mrs. Hazen S., 26
"Pingree's Potato Patch." *See* Community gardens
Pittsburgh, Pennsylvania, 31
Player, Cyril, 26
Plentywood, Montana, 88
*Political Science Quarterly,* 75
Portal, North Dakota, 83, 84
*Progress and Poverty,* 35
*Progressive Thought and Dawn of Equity,* 45, 47, 54

Rand, Peggy, 130-31
Reading, Pennsylvania, 31
Recent self-help activities
    assessment of, 138-40
    and barter clubs, 131-32
    and community gardens, 128-31
    and consumer-owned railroads, 134-36
    and cooperative stores, 132-34
    and intentional communities, 136-38
"Red River carts," 84-85
Red River Transportation Company, 84
Reunion Community, 117
*Review of Reviews,* 8
Richmond Union Passenger Railway, 96
Ridgely, Edwin Reed, 112, 113
Rochdale, England, 63
Rochdale Plan, 43-44. *See also* Cooperative stores
Rochester, New York, 32
Rock Lake, North Dakota, 92

Rolla, North Dakota, 85
Ruskin Co-operative Association, 113, 118

Sacramento, California, 130
Saint Louis, Missouri, 15, 31
Saint Paul, Minnnesota, 68–69, 70, 83, 85
Salvation Army, 18
Sandusky, Milan and Norwalk Railway, 98
San Francisco, California, 76
Saratoga, Kansas, 4
Sargent, Nebraska, 9
*Saturday Review,* 39
*Savannah News,* 38
Seattle, Washington, 15, 31, 32
*Seattle Intelligencer,* 34
Sedalia, Missouri, 43
Self-help. *See* Community gardens; Cooperative stores; Farmers' railroads; Intentional communities; Labor exchange(s); Recent self-help activities
Senior Gleaners, 130–31
Sheaf, Warren, 85–86
Sherman, John 14
Sherman Silver Purchase Act, 11–12
Simmons, P. A., 121, 122
Single-tax Club, 36
Soo Line Railroad, 87, 92, 93, 94
Sorenson, Rasmus, 90, 92
South Dakota, 5, 78
Spirit Fruit Society, 102
Sprague, Frank Julian, 96
Springfield, Missouri, 119
Starkweather, North Dakota, 90
Steinway, William, 32
Steubenville, Ohio, 19, 31
Stewart, Truman, 112
Stickney, A. B., 82–83
*Successful Farming,* 136
Sunkist Growers, 60
Superior, Wisconsin, 11
Swanson, Claude A., 13
Swedish Cooperative Association, 69
Syndicate buying. *See* Cooperative stores

T. V. Powderly Cooperative Association, 63
Tabegauche Park, Colorado, 122
Tappan, Austin, 102
Texas, Topolobampo and Pacific Railroad, 76–77
Thief River Falls, Minnesota, 93
Tivoli, New York, 137
Toledo, Fremont and Norwalk Railway, 98
Toledo, Ohio, 98. *See also* Labor exchange(s)
*Traveler from Altruria, A,* 103
*Trials and Triumph of Labor,* 42, 55
Thornbury, R. H., 48
Turner, James, 95
*Twentieth Century Farmer,* 10, 111

Union Pacific Railroad, 7
University Settlement House, 105
Utah Sugar Company, 65

Vacant Lots Cultivation Association, 36
Van Buren, Martin, 21–22
Vrooman, Walter, 105, 106

W. R. Grace, 139
Wabash Railroad, 82
Waite, Davis H., 15–16
Walder, Anne, 47
Wardall, Alonzo, 78
Warren, Josiah, 45
Washington, 53, 103
Waukesha, Wisconsin, 11
Wayland, Julius A., 114
*What Life Has Taught Me,* 123
Wilmington, Delaware, 36
Wilson-Gorman Act, 14
Winnipeg, Manitoba, 84
Winona, Minnesota, 31
Wisconsin, 11
Wright, Daniel, 137

Young, Coleman A., 129

Zumbrota, Minnesota, 70

H. ROGER GRANT is Professor of History at the University of Akron, Akron, Ohio. He is coeditor of *Years of Struggle: The Farm Diary of Elmer G. Powers, 1931–1936;* coauthor of *The Country Railroad Station in America;* and author of *Insurance Reform: Consumer Action in the Progressive Era.*